JANUARY

BACK TO BASICS

Start your year by building a rock-solid foundation. This month focuses on the fundamental skills every player needs - proper grip, ready position, footwork, and basic shot technique. When your basics feel reliable, you'll have the confidence to try new things all year long.

Pickleball
DAILY COMPANION

JANUARY 1

Whether you're picking up a paddle for the first time or returning to courts you love, start building success today. Before your first serve, take one deep breath and set a simple intention like 'have fun' or 'stay present.' This ritual will serve you well all year long.

Pickleball Daily Companion
A Year of Daily Pickleball Wisdom - Gift Edition

Author: Marjorie Keith

Illustrator: Alex Ryabintsev

Interior Layout: Joshua Egbeyale

Special thanks to Carolyn Lazar Butler for her unwavering support and to Maria Elshamy for believing in my vision and pushing this project forward.

ISBN: 979-8-9933374-0-1

First Edition
First published in the United States by **Terrain Vitality**

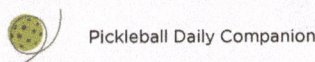

Pickleball Daily Companion

Welcome to your year of pickleball transformation!

Pickleball is the sport nobody saw coming - you show up to see what the fuss is about and leave with friendships, laughter, and a community that spans generations.

Inside, you'll find 365 daily tips organized by monthly themes - from mindset and positioning to advanced techniques and sportsmanship - to help you improve your game while deepening connections on and off the court.

Use this calendar to build confidence, enjoy more rallies, and embrace the friendships that make pickleball special.

With gratitude,

Written by Marji Keith
Illustrations by Alex Ryabintsev

Find more at pickleballdailycompanion.com

JANUARY 2

Serve deep with purpose. Aim for the back third of the court - near the baseline (the back boundary line) - to help your team take control of the point.

Coach's Tip:

Focus on your fundamentals. They are more valuable than flashy shots. When your basics feel reliable, you'll have confidence to try new things.

Pickleball
DAILY COMPANION

Pickleball Daily Companion

JANUARY 3

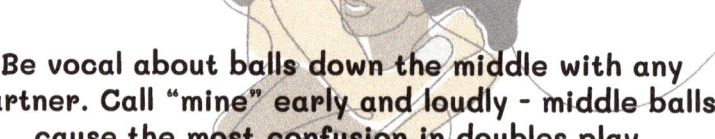

Be vocal about balls down the middle with any partner. Call "mine" early and loudly - middle balls cause the most confusion in doubles play.

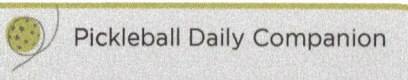

Pickleball
DAILY COMPANION

JANUARY 4

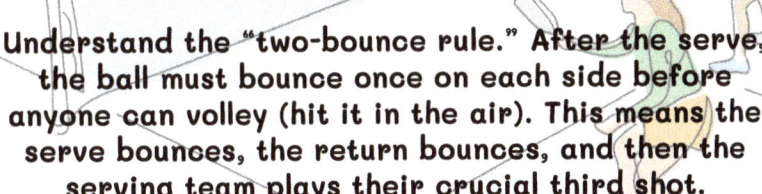

Understand the "two-bounce rule." After the serve, the ball must bounce once on each side before anyone can volley (hit it in the air). This means the serve bounces, the return bounces, and then the serving team plays their crucial third shot.

Coach's Tip:

Because the serving team can't volley yet, a soft third shot drop into the opponent's non-volley zone - also called the kitchen or NVZ - slows the point and gives the team time to move up to the net.

Pickleball
DAILY COMPANION

Pickleball Daily Companion

JANUARY 5

Patience wins points. Don't go for the hero shot - keep the ball in, place it well, and wait for the right opportunity. High-percentage play (safe, neutral shots) builds confidence.

JANUARY 6

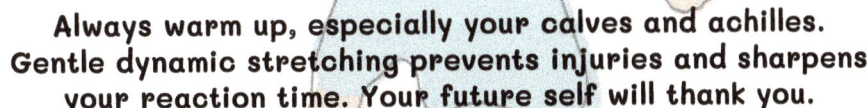

Always warm up, especially your calves and achilles.
Gentle dynamic stretching prevents injuries and sharpens
your reaction time. Your future self will thank you.

Pickleball
DAILY COMPANION

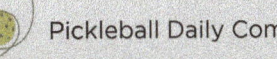

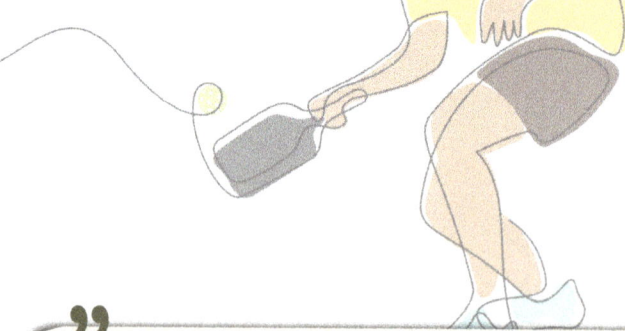

Hold your paddle like you're shaking hands with it. Not too tight, not too loose. This relaxed grip gives you better control and keeps your arm comfortable.

Coach's Tip:

Use a grip scale: soft (3/10) for dinking, firmer (7/10) for drives and volleys. Adjust your pressure for each shot type.

 Pickleball Daily Companion

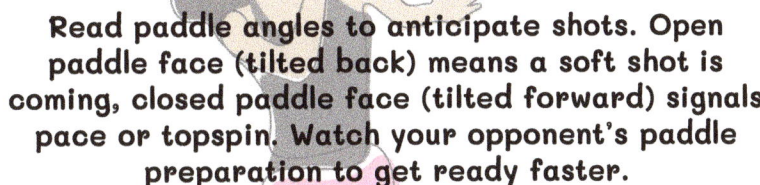

Read paddle angles to anticipate shots. Open paddle face (tilted back) means a soft shot is coming, closed paddle face (tilted forward) signals pace or topspin. Watch your opponent's paddle preparation to get ready faster.

JANUARY 9

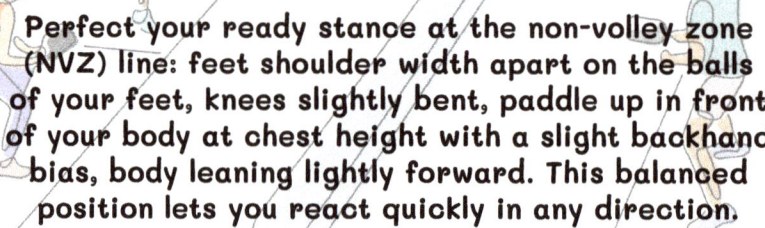

Perfect your ready stance at the non-volley zone (NVZ) line: feet shoulder width apart on the balls of your feet, knees slightly bent, paddle up in front of your body at chest height with a slight backhand bias, body leaning lightly forward. This balanced position lets you react quickly in any direction.

Pickleball
DAILY COMPANION

JANUARY 10

Keep your eyes on the ball from the moment it leaves your opponent's paddle until you hit it, and it leaves your paddle. Many players look away too early to see where their shot is going.

Coach's Tip:

By watching the ball completely through contact, your natural hand-eye coordination will guide placement more accurately.

Pickleball
DAILY COMPANION

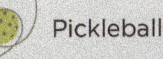
Pickleball Daily Companion

JANUARY 11

Always hit the ball in front of your body for improved control and power. Your paddle should make contact while the ball is still out in front of you, rather than waiting until it's beside or behind your body. This contact point works for all shots - NVZ volleys, baseline groundstrokes, and everything in between.

Coach's Tip:

Develop a quick mental reset routine for pressure moments. Take a breath, focus on one simple cue like 'contact in front,' and commit to that thought.

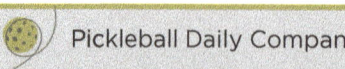 Pickleball Daily Companion

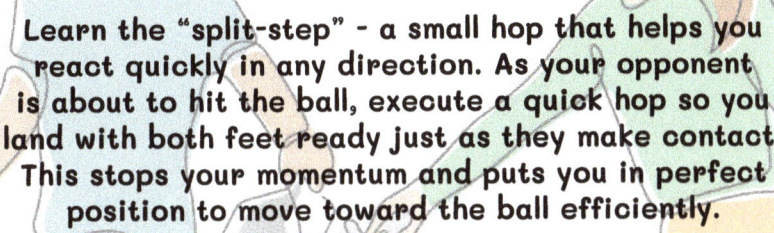

Learn the "split-step" - a small hop that helps you react quickly in any direction. As your opponent is about to hit the ball, execute a quick hop so you land with both feet ready just as they make contact. This stops your momentum and puts you in perfect position to move toward the ball efficiently.

Pickleball
DAILY COMPANION

Pickleball Daily Companion

JANUARY 13

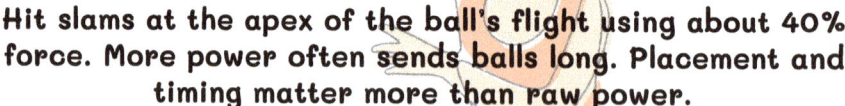

Hit slams at the apex of the ball's flight using about 40% force. More power often sends balls long. Placement and timing matter more than raw power.

JANUARY 14

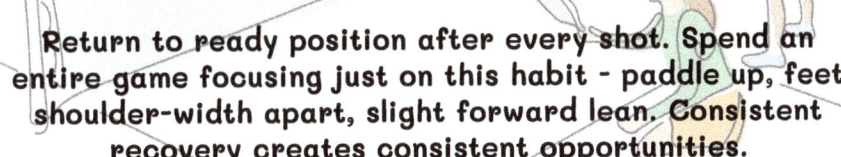

Return to ready position after every shot. Spend an entire game focusing just on this habit - paddle up, feet shoulder-width apart, slight forward lean. Consistent recovery creates consistent opportunities.

Coach's Tip:

A balanced ready stance creates multiple shot options while maintaining defensive coverage. Return to this position after every shot and you will have more time to react.

Pickleball
DAILY COMPANION

JANUARY 15

When your partner gets pulled wide, immediately shuffle-step to cover the open middle, then return to your position once they recover. This automatic coverage prevents easy winners down the line.

Coach's Tip:

The heart of good teamwork is the no-surprise rule. When you're predictable to your partner, you're unpredictable to your opponents.

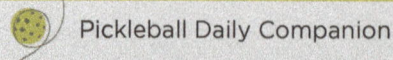

JANUARY 16

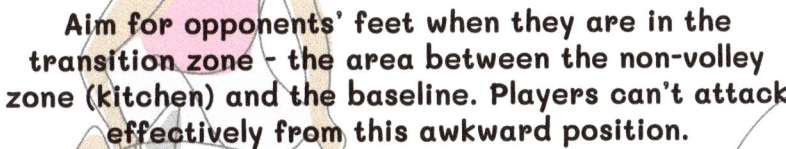

Aim for opponents' feet when they are in the transition zone - the area between the non-volley zone (kitchen) and the baseline. Players can't attack effectively from this awkward position.

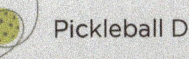

To sharpen your serve, keep your head down and your eyes on the ball - right through contact - longer than you think. Watch the paddle meet the ball, then silently count "one" before looking up.

Pickleball Daily Companion

JANUARY 18

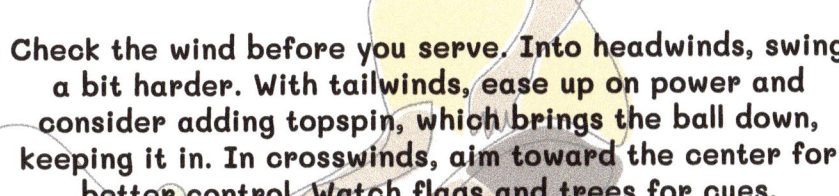

Check the wind before you serve. Into headwinds, swing a bit harder. With tailwinds, ease up on power and consider adding topspin, which brings the ball down, keeping it in. In crosswinds, aim toward the center for better control. Watch flags and trees for cues.

JANUARY 19

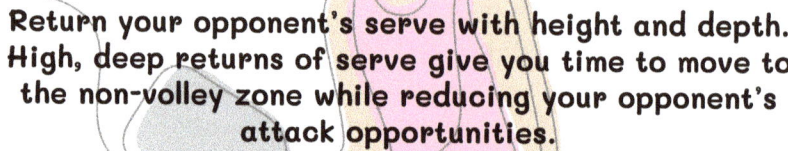

Return your opponent's serve with height and depth. High, deep returns of serve give you time to move to the non-volley zone while reducing your opponent's attack opportunities.

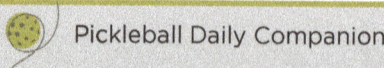

Wear shoes made specifically for pickleball - your ankles, knees, and back will thank you. Pickleball requires quick side-to-side movements that running shoes aren't designed for. Court shoes provide the stability and grip you need to move safely and confidently on the court.

Pickleball
DAILY COMPANION

Punch, don't swing, in fast exchanges at the net. Use short, firm strokes with minimal backswing - as if pushing your paddle or punching through the ball. This works better than big swings when there's no time.

JANUARY 22

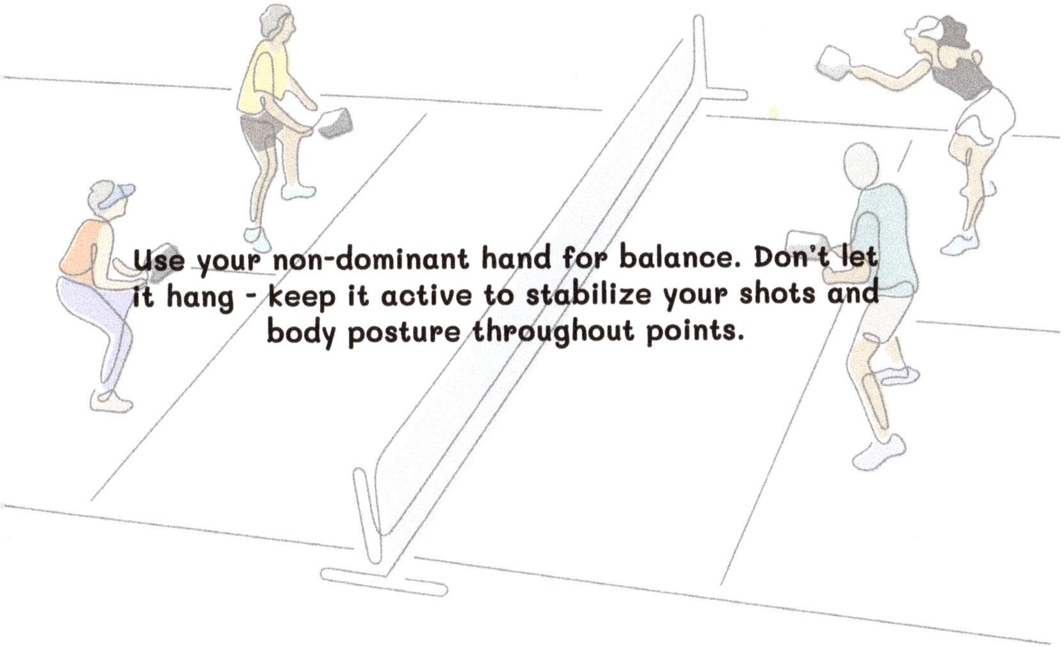

Use your non-dominant hand for balance. Don't let it hang – keep it active to stabilize your shots and body posture throughout points.

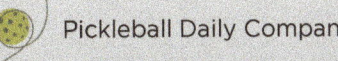

New to pickleball? The community is incredibly welcoming! Look for beginner-friendly play at local courts, check social media for area groups, or ask recreation centers about intro sessions. Many areas have scheduling apps showing skill levels. The friendships you'll make can be as valuable as the exercise.

JANUARY 24

Practice the art of letting out balls go. Watch the ball's trajectory early - balls hit with an upward swing often sail long, especially when opponents are stretched or off-balance. Trust your judgment and resist the urge to chase every ball.

Coach's Tip:

Most players give away too many points by hitting balls that were heading out. Learning to let them go takes practice, practice, practice until resisting becomes instinct.

Pickleball
DAILY COMPANION

 Pickleball Daily Companion

JANUARY 25

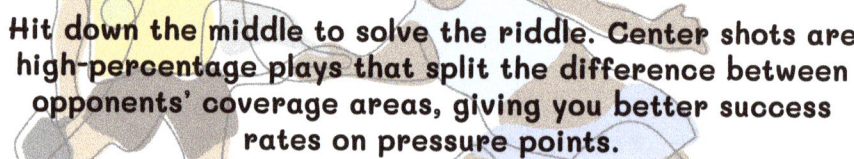

Hit down the middle to solve the riddle. Center shots are high-percentage plays that split the difference between opponents' coverage areas, giving you better success rates on pressure points.

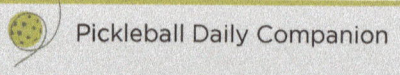

JANUARY 26

Take full breaths between points to reset concentration and ensure oxygen flow to the muscles and brain. This simple habit improves decision-making and reduces tension.

Coach's Tip:

Think of routines as your personal ritual for excellence. That moment of preparation tells your brain it's time to focus.

Pickleball
DAILY COMPANION

 Pickleball Daily Companion

JANUARY 27

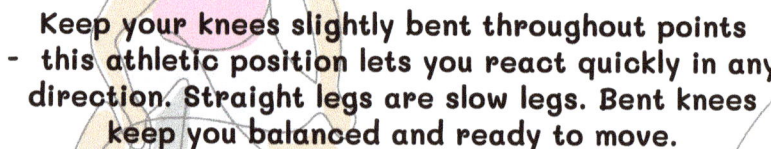

Keep your knees slightly bent throughout points - this athletic position lets you react quickly in any direction. Straight legs are slow legs. Bent knees keep you balanced and ready to move.

JANUARY 28

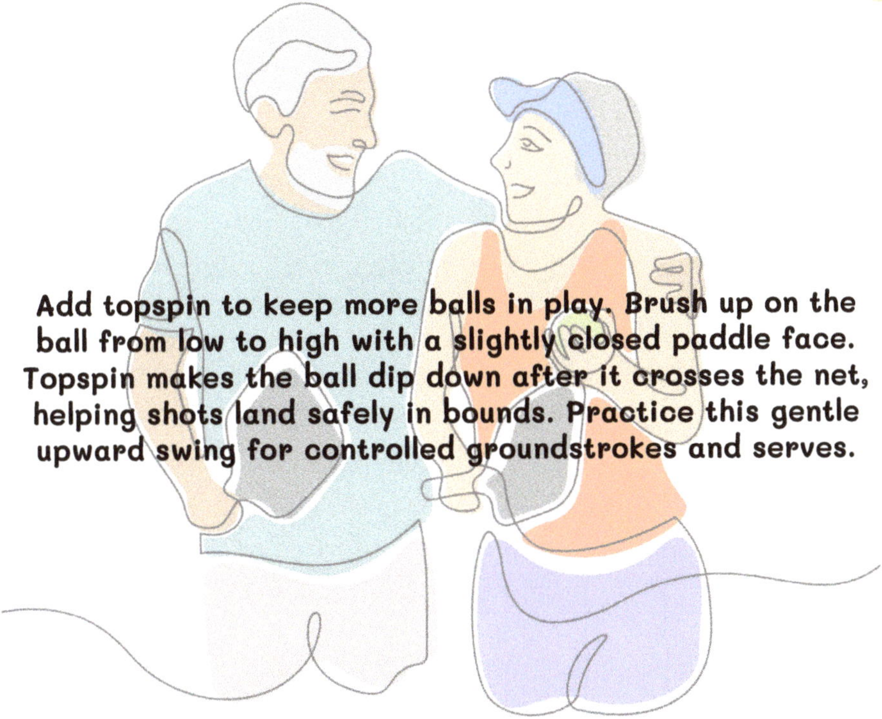

Add topspin to keep more balls in play. Brush up on the ball from low to high with a slightly closed paddle face. Topspin makes the ball dip down after it crosses the net, helping shots land safely in bounds. Practice this gentle upward swing for controlled groundstrokes and serves.

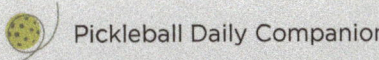

JANUARY 29

When dinking, newer players should aim for the middle of the NVZ to maximize margin for error and keep balls unattackable. As your skills advance, aim for the outsides of your opponent's feet to stretch their reach and create openings.

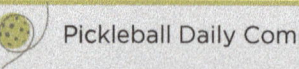

Pickleball Daily Companion

Pickleball
DAILY COMPANION

Position yourself strategically to receive serves. Stand about 2-3 feet behind the baseline, feet shoulder-width apart, with your paddle ready in front. This gives you time to react to hard serves while allowing you to move forward on soft serves.

JANUARY 31

Practice one fundamental skill for 5 minutes before playing today. Whether it's serves, dinks, or footwork - focused practice builds reliable habits that bring lasting joy.

 Pickleball Daily Companion

FEBRUARY

Your mental game is just as important as your physical skills. Learn to stay calm under pressure, bounce back from mistakes, and develop the positive self-talk that transforms good players into great ones. A strong mindset makes every other skill easier to develop

FEBRUARY 1

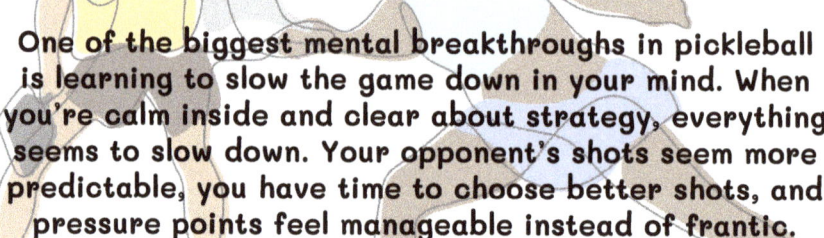

One of the biggest mental breakthroughs in pickleball is learning to slow the game down in your mind. When you're calm inside and clear about strategy, everything seems to slow down. Your opponent's shots seem more predictable, you have time to choose better shots, and pressure points feel manageable instead of frantic.

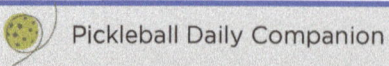

FEBRUARY 2

Your self-talk creates your reality. If you say, "I always miss this shot," your brain accepts this as fact and performs accordingly. Replace negative predictions with encouraging statements.

Pickleball
DAILY COMPANION

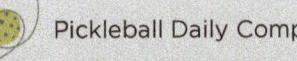

Pickleball Daily Companion

FEBRUARY 3

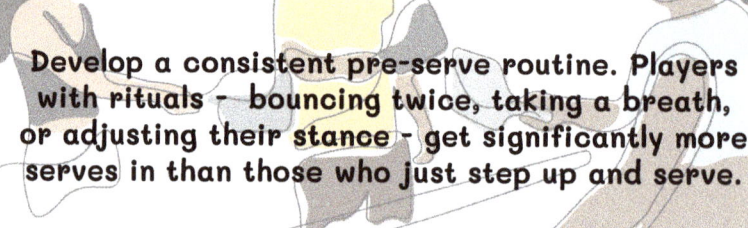

Develop a consistent pre-serve routine. Players with rituals - bouncing twice, taking a breath, or adjusting their stance - get significantly more serves in than those who just step up and serve.

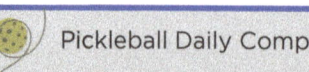

Pickleball
DAILY COMPANION

FEBRUARY 4

Develop a bounce-back mentality that treats every point as a fresh start. Don't let excellent shots make you overconfident or mistakes make you tentative. Reset mentally between every single point, staying emotionally neutral and strategically sharp.

FEBRUARY 5

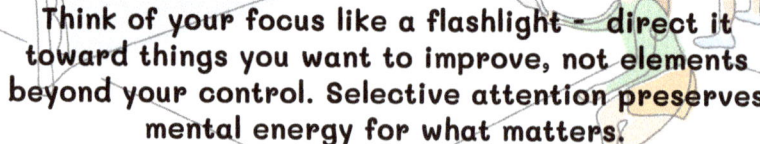

Think of your focus like a flashlight – direct it toward things you want to improve, not elements beyond your control. Selective attention preserves mental energy for what matters.

 Pickleball Daily Companion

FEBRUARY 6

Consider pickleball as both physical exercise and mental training. Skills like staying calm under pressure and bouncing back from mistakes transfer to life beyond the court.

Coach's Tip:

Players at ease with their minds have an advantage over those who merely know their paddle. Mental resilience often determines outcomes.

Pickleball
DAILY COMPANION

Pickleball Daily Companion

FEBRUARY 7

Train your brain to notice what's improving, not just what's wrong. When your serves feel more consistent or you stay calm after errors, celebrate these mental victories. Your brain needs positive feedback to build genuine confidence - give it the fuel it craves.

Coach's Tip:

Your mind is your most important piece of equipment. Keep it well-oiled through consistent mental routines and positive self-talk.

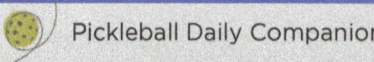

Pickleball Daily Companion

Pickleball
DAILY COMPANION

FEBRUARY 8

Know that some days feel better than others.
Natural performance fluctuations happen to
all players, even professionals. Embrace the
variability with kindness to yourself.

Pickleball
DAILY COMPANION

Pickleball Daily Companion

FEBRUARY 9

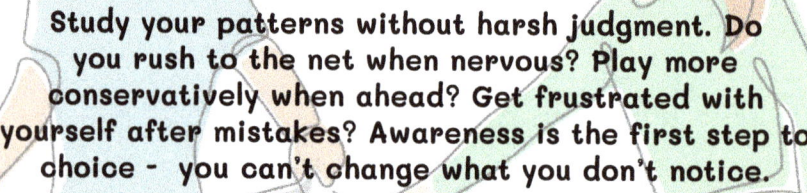

Study your patterns without harsh judgment. Do you rush to the net when nervous? Play more conservatively when ahead? Get frustrated with yourself after mistakes? Awareness is the first step to choice - you can't change what you don't notice.

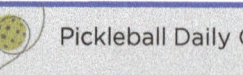
Pickleball Daily Companion

Pickleball
DAILY COMPANION

FEBRUARY 10

Embrace the power of "yet" in your self-talk. Replace "I'm a bad server" with "I haven't learned consistent serving yet." This simple word transforms limitations into possibilities.

Coach's Tip:

Your game evolves constantly. Stay open to growth rather than labeling yourself with permanent limitations.

Pickleball
DAILY COMPANION

Pickleball Daily Companion

FEBRUARY 11

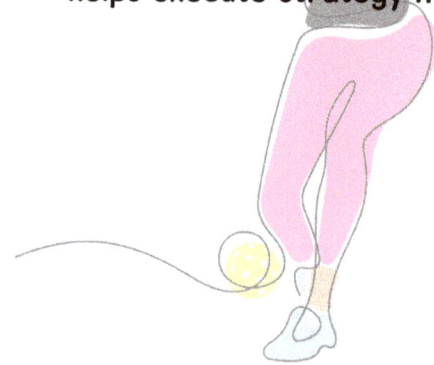

Use your pre-serve routine to set specific intentions. Think "deep and patient" or "aim cross-court to their backhand." Mental programming helps execute strategy instead of just reacting.

FEBRUARY 12

Consider a 'fresh start' mindset between games. Take 30 seconds to consciously release the last game - good or bad - and set a clear intention for the next one. Ask yourself: "What energy do I want to bring to this game?" Players who reset well enjoy every game more.

Coach's Tip:

The pause between games is your chance to refresh your outlook. A simple intention like 'stay patient' or 'have fun' can transform your next game.

Pickleball
DAILY COMPANION

Pickleball Daily Companion

FEBRUARY 13

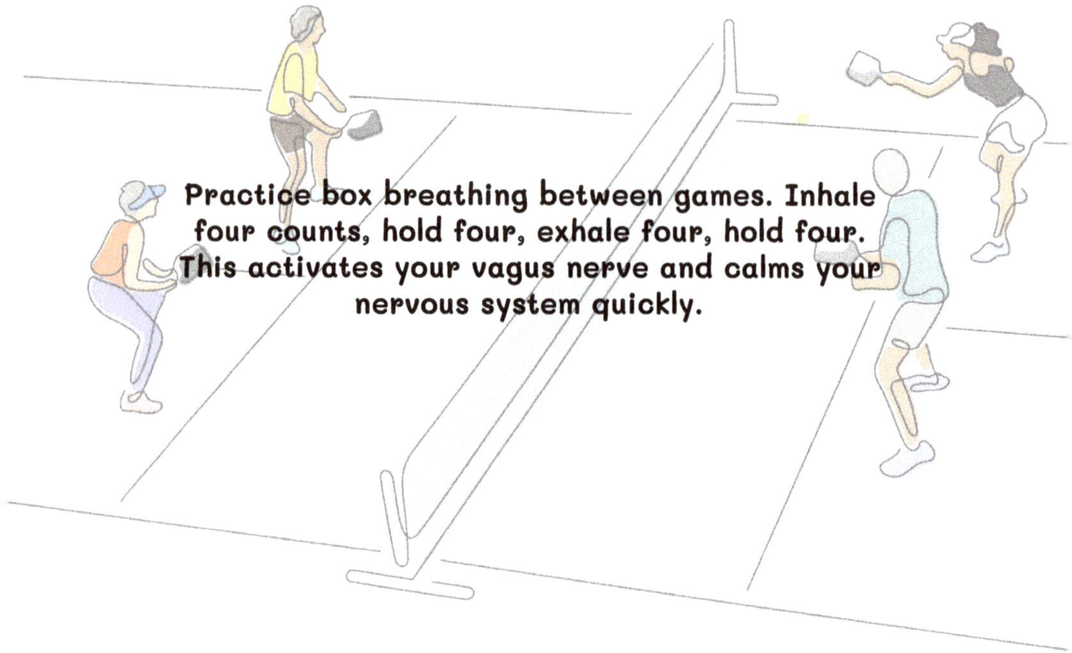

Practice box breathing between games. Inhale four counts, hold four, exhale four, hold four. This activates your vagus nerve and calms your nervous system quickly.

 Pickleball Daily Companion

FEBRUARY 14

Discover your partner's pickleball love language - technical tips, confidence boosts, or quiet focus. Give them what helps them play their best, not what feels natural to you.

Pickleball
DAILY COMPANION

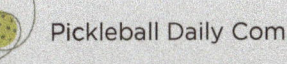
Pickleball Daily Companion

FEBRUARY 15

Direct energy toward what you control: shot selection, footwork, and attitude. Your opponent's behavior, line calls, and wind are beyond your reach - let them go.

Coach's Tip:

In life, like in pickleball, you're responsible for what you send from your side of the net.

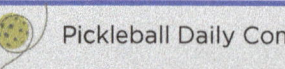
Pickleball Daily Companion

FEBRUARY 16

Build trust through consistent encouragement while reading your partner's energy level. Notice when they're tense, confident, or frustrated, then adjust your communication style. Simple phrases like "good try" combined with energy awareness creates mental safety for smart risks.

 Pickleball Daily Companion

FEBRUARY 17

Consider signing up for your first tournament - they're surprisingly low-key and fun! Most have beginner divisions with supportive players. It's a great way to meet new people and test your skills in a friendly environment.

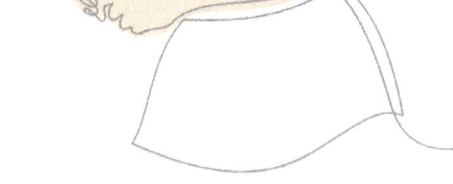

Coach's Tip:
Tournaments reveal your true mental game because you can't hide from pressure. Use them as laboratories to test your mindset work and your strokes.

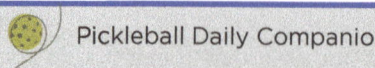
Pickleball Daily Companion

Pickleball
DAILY COMPANION

FEBRUARY 18

Practice contact point awareness by calling out "now!" when your paddle touches the ball during drills. This builds precise timing and mental focus on the moment of contact.

FEBRUARY 19

Develop mental flexibility for pressure situations.
Create simple phrases like "one point at a time"
or "trust my shots" that instantly refocus your
mind during crucial moments.

FEBRUARY 20

Handle questionable line calls with grace and strategy. Give opponents the benefit of doubt on close calls, call your own faults honestly, and remember that good sportsmanship often influences future calls in your favor.

Coach's Tip:

Your mental composure during disputes sets the tone for the entire match.

Pickleball
DAILY COMPANION

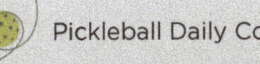

FEBRUARY 21

Follow through in the direction you want the ball to go, then return to ready position. Hold your finish momentarily to reinforce proper technique and build muscle memory.

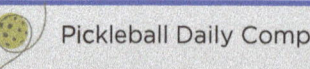
Pickleball Daily Companion

Pickleball
DAILY COMPANION

FEBRUARY 22

Practice a mindful partnership by tuning into your teammate's rhythm. When they're playing conservatively, match their patience. When they're off rhythm, slow the ball down to help.

Coach's Tip:
Excellent partners don't just play well together - they recover well together. How you respond after mistakes matters most.

Pickleball
DAILY COMPANION

 Pickleball Daily Companion

FEBRUARY 23

Transform nervous energy into focused excitement. Butterflies before important points mean you care - channel that energy into sharper concentration rather than fighting it.

 Pickleball Daily Companion

 Pickleball
DAILY COMPANION

FEBRUARY 24

After each game, identify three things that went well - maybe your footwork, a great rally, or staying positive. This trains your brain to notice progress and builds authentic confidence.

Pickleball
DAILY COMPANION

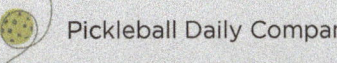

FEBRUARY 25

Watch for mental fatigue signals: rushed decisions, tightness, or negative thoughts. When you notice these, take an extra breath and simplify your game plan.

Coach's Tip:
Mind fatigue hits before physical fatigue. When your decision making gets sloppy, that's your brain asking for a reset, not your body asking for a break.

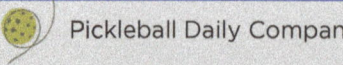

Pickleball Daily Companion

Pickleball
DAILY COMPANION

Adjust your grip pressure mid-rally based on shot type. A lighter grip for soft shots, a firmer grip for drives. This adaptability prevents arm fatigue and improves shot variety throughout long matches.

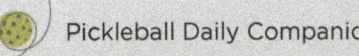

Pickleball Daily Companion

FEBRUARY 27

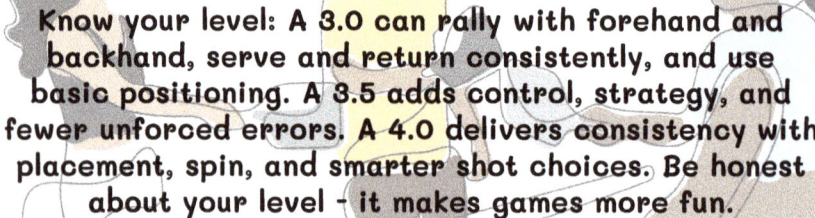

Know your level: A 3.0 can rally with forehand and backhand, serve and return consistently, and use basic positioning. A 3.5 adds control, strategy, and fewer unforced errors. A 4.0 delivers consistency with placement, spin, and smarter shot choices. Be honest about your level - it makes games more fun.

Pickleball
DAILY COMPANION

FEBRUARY 28

Keep good energy flowing by communicating clearly, avoiding unsolicited advice on court, projecting positive body language, making generous line calls, and rotating off quickly when others are waiting. Respecting these unwritten rules keeps pickleball fun for everyone.

Coach's Tip:

Smile, smile, smile - and laugh a lot.

Pickleball
DAILY COMPANION

Pickleball Daily Companion

MARCH

Discover where to stand, when to move, and how to read the game like a chess master. Court positioning wins more points than power shots. This month you'll learn to see patterns, anticipate opponents, and always be in the right place at the right time.

MARCH 1

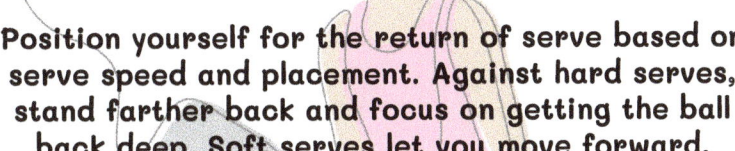

Position yourself for the return of serve based on serve speed and placement. Against hard serves, stand farther back and focus on getting the ball back deep. Soft serves let you move forward.

Pickleball
DAILY COMPANION

MARCH 2

Court spacing is like dancing with your partner. Too close and you'll step on each other's toes. Too far and you'll leave gaps for opponents to exploit.

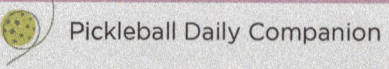

Your feet tell the truth about your preparation. If you're frequently lunging or reaching, you're probably not moving your feet enough before the shot. Small shuffle steps make a world of difference.

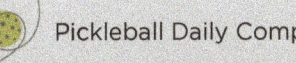

MARCH 4

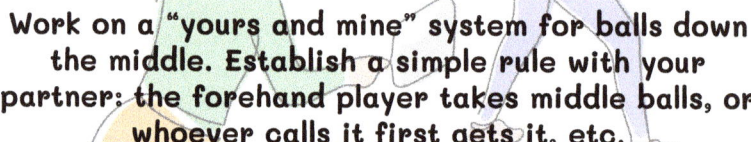

Work on a "yours and mine" system for balls down the middle. Establish a simple rule with your partner: the forehand player takes middle balls, or whoever calls it first gets it, etc.

Coach's Tip:

Don't just wing it - even in recreational play, it's worth having a quick agreement with your partner before or during the game. That avoids hesitation and missed balls.

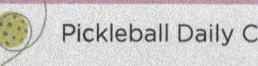

Pickleball
DAILY COMPANION

Take the ball early when possible - time and position win points as much as power. Hitting balls on the rise or at their peak gives opponents less time to prepare and puts you in control of the rally's tempo.

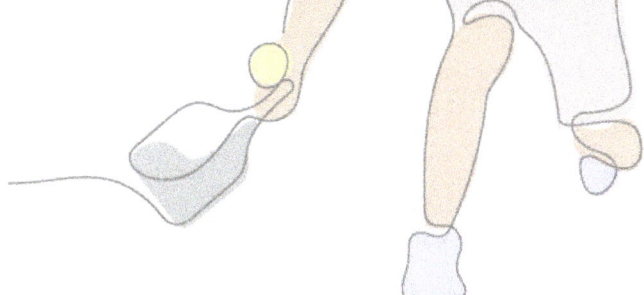

Pickleball
DAILY COMPANION

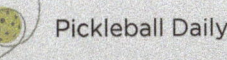

Here's the kitchen rule made simple: You can step into the NVZ anytime you want - just don't hit the ball out of the air while you're in there. Let the ball bounce first, then hit it. The tricky part? If you volley (hit in the air) from outside the NVZ but your momentum carries you in afterward, that's still a fault. Plant your feet before volleying near the line.

Coach's Tip:

Knowledge of the rules is fuel for confidence.

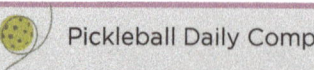

MARCH 7

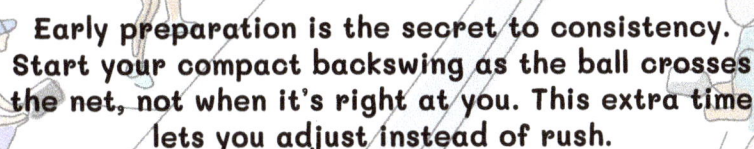

Early preparation is the secret to consistency. Start your compact backswing as the ball crosses the net, not when it's right at you. This extra time lets you adjust instead of rush.

> **Coach's Tip:**
> Watch professionals play - they're in position and preparing their stroke while the ball is still on the other side of the court.

Pickleball
DAILY COMPANION

Pickleball Daily Companion

MARCH 8

Learn to read your partner like a book. Notice their patterns - do they favor their forehand? Do they get tentative when pulled wide? Great partners anticipate each other's moves.

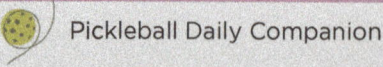

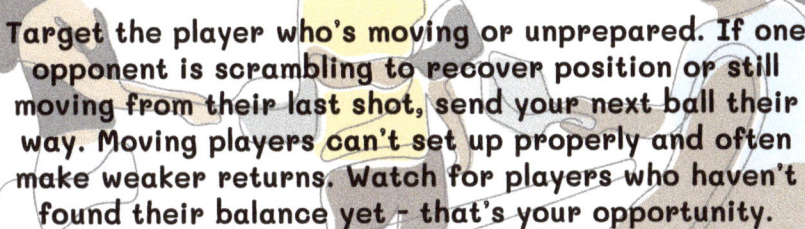

Target the player who's moving or unprepared. If one opponent is scrambling to recover position or still moving from their last shot, send your next ball their way. Moving players can't set up properly and often make weaker returns. Watch for players who haven't found their balance yet - that's your opportunity.

Pickleball
DAILY COMPANION

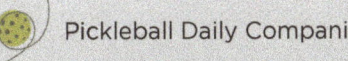

MARCH 10

Learn the transition zone fundamentals. This area between baseline and NVZ/kitchen requires quick decisions - be ready to move forward after good shots or back after weak ones.

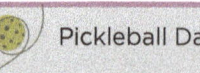

Pickleball
DAILY COMPANION

MARCH 11

Balance risk and reward based on score. When you're ahead 10-7, play the point as though it was 7-10. When it's close, stick with high-percentage positioning and shot selection.

 Pickleball Daily Companion

MARCH 12

Learn to identify and target opponent weaknesses through positioning. Watch their paddle hand - their backhand is the opposite side. Right-handed players struggle with balls to their left side; lefties struggle on their right. Position yourself to hit more balls to that weaker side, especially when they're stretched or off-balance.

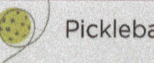
Pickleball Daily Companion

Pickleball
DAILY COMPANION

MARCH 13

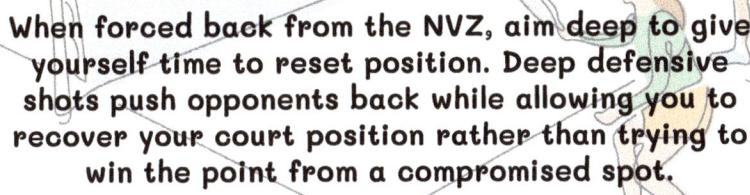

When forced back from the NVZ, aim deep to give yourself time to reset position. Deep defensive shots push opponents back while allowing you to recover your court position rather than trying to win the point from a compromised spot.

MARCH 14

Position yourself based on your partner's shot quality. After they hit a strong shot, move up slightly in anticipation of a weak return. After weak shots, prepare to defend by staying back.

"

Coach's Tip:

Positioning is like playing chess with your feet. Every step should either cut off an opponent's option or create a new option for you.

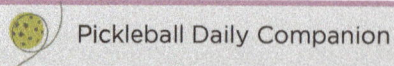 Pickleball Daily Companion

 Pickleball
DAILY COMPANION

Follow the ball and keep your paddle tilted towards it. When the ball is on your opponents' side of the net, both you and your partner shift toward whichever side the ball is on. If the ball goes to the left side, slide left while maintaining your spacing. This positioning puts you in the best spot to handle their most likely returns.

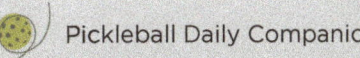

Pickleball Daily Companion

MARCH 16

Use interference calls as positioning resets. When external factors disrupt play, calling "replay" gives everyone a chance to reposition safely and fairly.

Coach's Tip:

Maybe it will help to remember how lucky we are to hit a plastic ball and laugh.

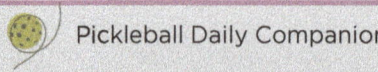

Pickleball Daily Companion

Pickleball
DAILY COMPANION

Learn to read court-positioning tells throughout the match. Notice where opponents stand during different scores, when they're tired versus fresh, and how they position when ahead versus behind. Use this information to anticipate their strategy.

MARCH 18

Take balls out of the air at the non-volley zone whenever you can - it gives opponents less time to react. But if you need more time to set up a good shot, let it bounce first. Trust your instincts about when you're ready.

Use court positioning to control rally pace. Stand closer to the NVZ when you want to speed up exchanges, position deeper when you want to slow the pace and build points patiently.

When opponents hit an aggressive shot, both you and your partner should move slightly toward the attacking ball. Don't abandon your positions completely - just shift your weight and lean toward where the pressure is coming from.

Coach's Tip:

Simple rule: their paddles go up, yours goes down. When opponents prepare to attack from above, your low paddle position gives you the best angle to defend and reset.

 Pickleball Daily Companion

MARCH 21

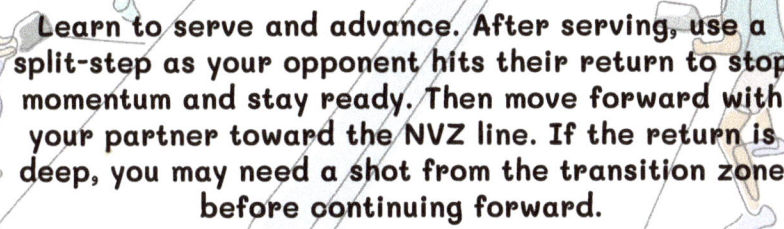

Learn to serve and advance. After serving, use a split-step as your opponent hits their return to stop momentum and stay ready. Then move forward with your partner toward the NVZ line. If the return is deep, you may need a shot from the transition zone before continuing forward.

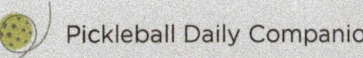

MARCH 22

Wait until your opponents are ready before serving. This courtesy creates respect, but also ensures everyone is properly positioned for safe, fair play.

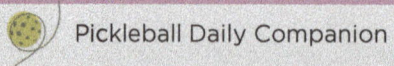

Pickleball Daily Companion

Pickleball
DAILY COMPANION

Use the two-bounce rule to create opportunities.
Because the receiver must let your serve bounce,
a deep serve can keep them from rushing the net
right away. After their return, they may be stuck
in the transition zone - your chance to drop,
drive, or target their feet.

 Pickleball Daily Companion

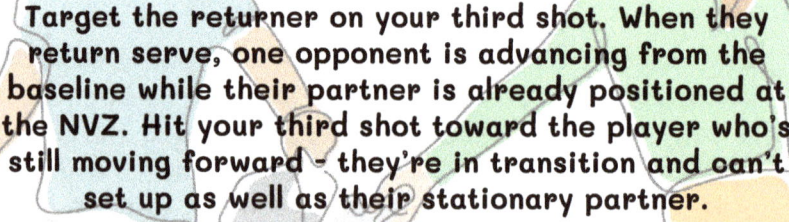

Target the returner on your third shot. When they return serve, one opponent is advancing from the baseline while their partner is already positioned at the NVZ. Hit your third shot toward the player who's still moving forward - they're in transition and can't set up as well as their stationary partner.

Pickleball
DAILY COMPANION

Handle balls hit behind you with footwork rather than reaching. Take one small step backward to get your body behind the ball, then turn your shoulders to face your target. This creates a comfortable hitting position instead of an awkward reach.

Coach's Tip:

A relaxed swing from good position beats a rushed one while stretching.

Pickleball Daily Companion

Imagine an invisible elastic band connecting you and your partner. When they move wide, you move with them in the same direction to maintain proper spacing. When they recover, you both snap back to balanced court coverage. This connection keeps you moving as one unit.

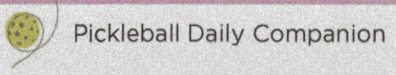
Pickleball Daily Companion

MARCH 27

Develop "court sense" - that intuitive feeling for where you should be without constantly looking around. This awareness comes from focused practice and observation.

Pickleball
DAILY COMPANION

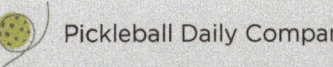

Pickleball Daily Companion

Use positioning to disguise your intentions. Stand in similar spots for different shots so opponents can't read your strategy until the last moment.

Pickleball Daily Companion

MARCH 29

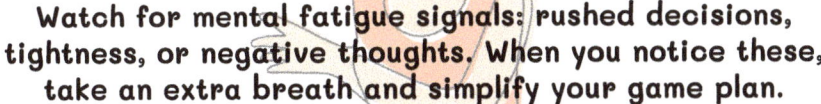

Watch for mental fatigue signals: rushed decisions,
tightness, or negative thoughts. When you notice these,
take an extra breath and simplify your game plan.

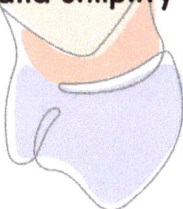

Pickleball
DAILY COMPANION

 Pickleball Daily Companion

If practicing on your own, try hitting third shot drops to specific NVZ corners. Start close to the net, then gradually move back to the baseline. Drilling builds muscle memory fast, and it's something you can even do alone.

Notice when positioning becomes more natural. When court awareness feels automatic, you can focus your mental energy on strategy, reading opponents, and making smart shot choices.

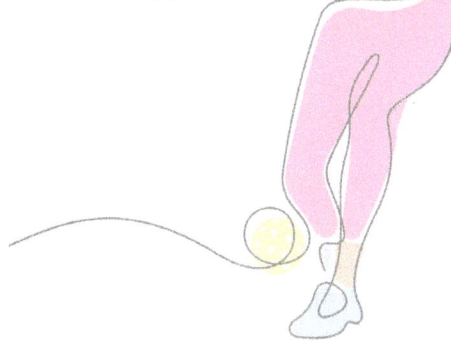

APRIL

Every opponent is different. Every day feels different. Learn to adjust your game plan mid-match, recover quickly from tough points, and turn challenges into opportunities. Flexible players have more fun and win more games.

Adapt your ball tracking to different shot types. Topspin dips fast, slice floats and curves, drives come straight. Learning to read these patterns early helps you adjust your positioning and timing.

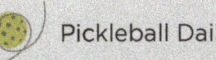
Pickleball Daily Companion

APRIL 2

Recover quickly using hand signals or quick words like "reset," "switch" and "go" for lobs to regroup with your partner after scrambled points. These cues make mid-game pivots smoother.

Coach's Tip:
Resilient partners know that recovering from compromised situations is the heart of doubles play.

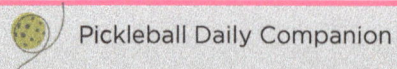
Pickleball Daily Companion

APRIL 3

You have more time than you realize, so there's no need to rush. That split second of panic when the ball comes your way? Breathe through it. You usually have enough time to set your feet, prepare your paddle, and make a deliberate choice.

Coach's Tip:

When you feel rushed, take a breath and trust your preparation. Your body knows what to do when your fundamentals are strong and your mind stays calm.

Pickleball
DAILY COMPANION

Pickleball Daily Companion

APRIL 4

Embrace the next-ball mentality. After any error or great opponent shot, immediately think "next-ball." This mental reset prevents dwelling on the past point and keeps you present.

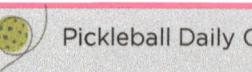

Pickleball
DAILY COMPANION

APRIL 5

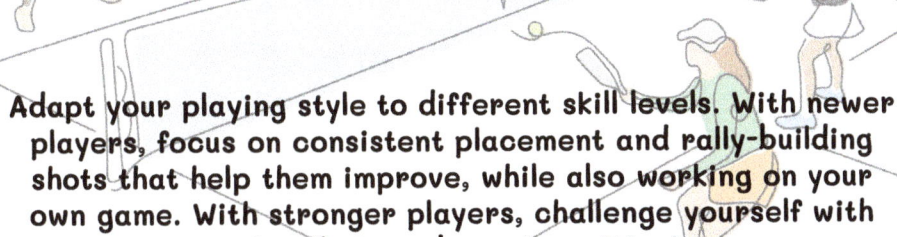

Adapt your playing style to different skill levels. With newer players, focus on consistent placement and rally-building shots that help them improve, while also working on your own game. With stronger players, challenge yourself with precise shots and smart positioning.

Pickleball
DAILY COMPANION

Pickleball Daily Companion

APRIL 6

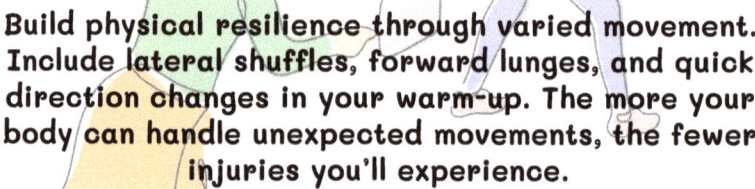

Build physical resilience through varied movement.
Include lateral shuffles, forward lunges, and quick
direction changes in your warm-up. The more your
body can handle unexpected movements, the fewer
injuries you'll experience.

 Pickleball Daily Companion

APRIL 7

Evaluate your response to different playing styles. Notice your reactions to bangers versus dinkers, aggressive versus patient players. Modify your game plans based on opponents' tendencies.

Pickleball
DAILY COMPANION

Pickleball Daily Companion

APRIL 8

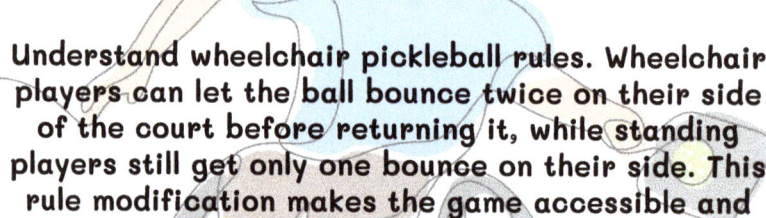

Understand wheelchair pickleball rules. Wheelchair players can let the ball bounce twice on their side of the court before returning it, while standing players still get only one bounce on their side. This rule modification makes the game accessible and competitive for players using wheelchairs.

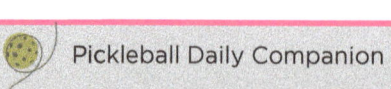

APRIL 9

Patience wins more points than you realize. Instead of rushing to end rallies, let them develop naturally. Hit some solid, placement-focused shots before looking for your first aggressive opportunity.

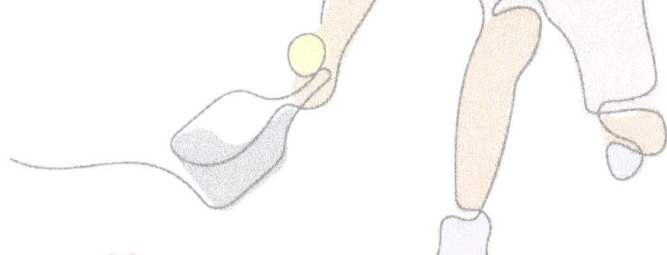

Coach's Tip:

Forced winners become unforced errors, but patient sequences create genuine openings you can attack with confidence.

Pickleball
DAILY COMPANION

Pickleball Daily Companion

APRIL 10

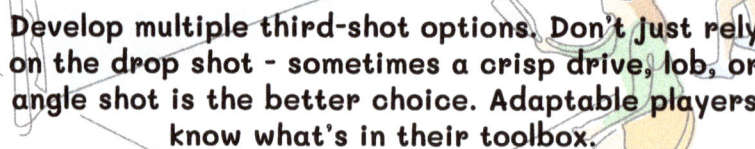

Develop multiple third-shot options. Don't just rely on the drop shot - sometimes a crisp drive, lob, or angle shot is the better choice. Adaptable players know what's in their toolbox.

APRIL 11

Whether you make mistakes or hit great shots, return to neutral quickly. Mental extremes cloud judgment for the next point. Taking a breath and focusing forward prevents past points from affecting future opportunities.

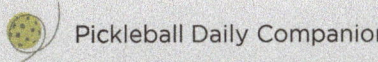
Pickleball Daily Companion

APRIL 12

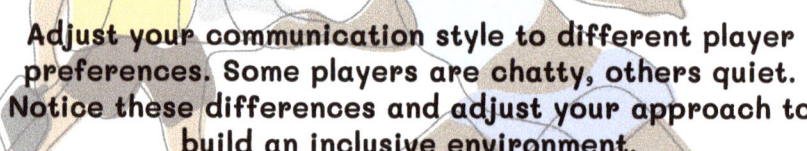

Adjust your communication style to different player preferences. Some players are chatty, others quiet. Notice these differences and adjust your approach to build an inclusive environment.

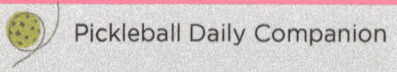
Pickleball Daily Companion

Pickleball
DAILY COMPANION

APRIL 13

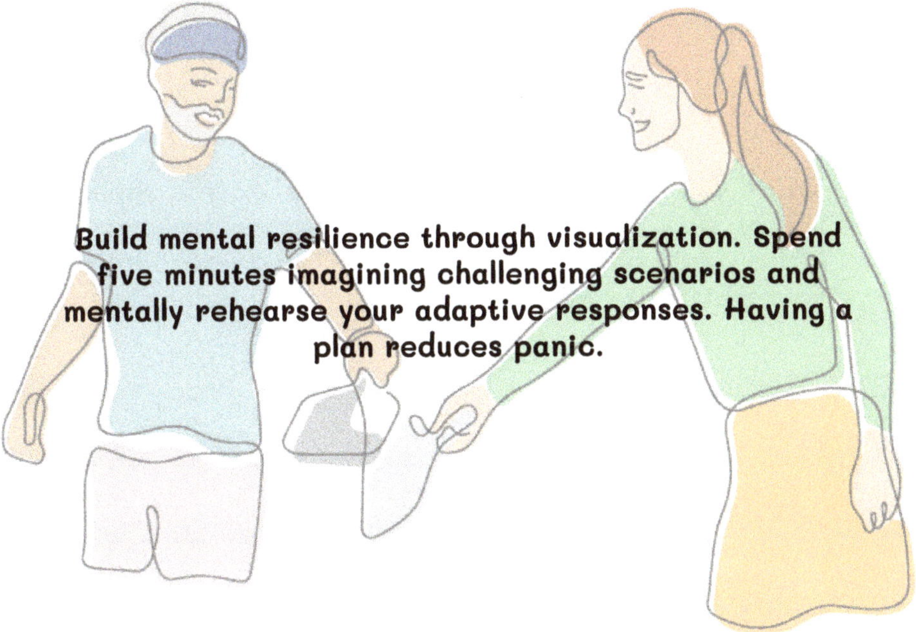

Build mental resilience through visualization. Spend five minutes imagining challenging scenarios and mentally rehearse your adaptive responses. Having a plan reduces panic.

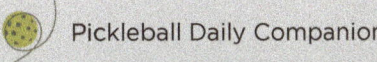

APRIL 14

Notice your patterns under pressure. Do you speed up or slow down when stressed? Do you become more aggressive or conservative? Understanding your patterns helps you try different approaches.

Coach's Tip:

Try recording a few points to observe your choices under pressure. Awareness is the first step to changing habits and making smarter decisions during matches.

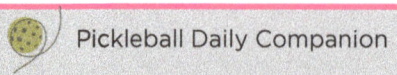

Pickleball Daily Companion

Pickleball
DAILY COMPANION

APRIL 15

Practice the art of changing pace. The ability to speed up or slow down the ball disrupts your opponents' rhythm and keeps them guessing. Practice hitting the same shot at three different speeds.

Coach's Tip:

Change pace mid-rally to disrupt rhythm. Add a soft ball during fast exchanges - tempo changes often force pop-ups or unforced errors.

Pickleball
DAILY COMPANION

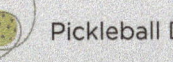

Pickleball Daily Companion

APRIL 16

Develop quick recovery communication with any partner. Simple calls like "got it" when covering for them help any partnership flow better, even if you just met.

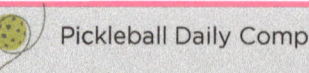

APRIL 17

Learn to identify and pressure opponent weaknesses. If someone struggles with backhands, wait for the right moment when they're off-balance. Timing your adjustments maximizes impact.

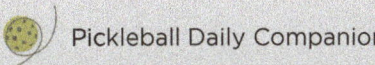

Develop comfort with discomfort. Learn to perform well even when things feel off - bad bounces, unusual opponents, windy conditions. Embrace the game's imperfections instead of fighting them.

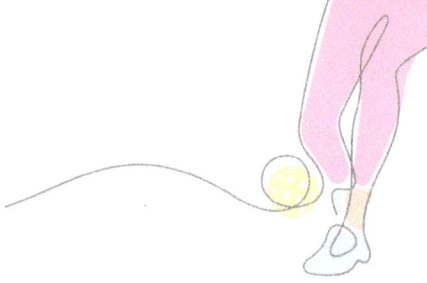

APRIL 19

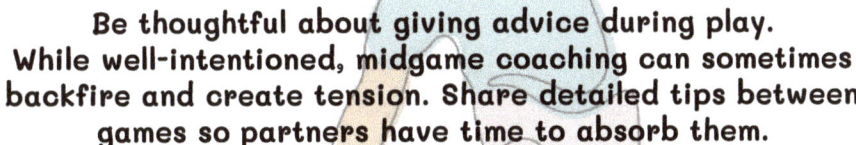

Be thoughtful about giving advice during play. While well-intentioned, midgame coaching can sometimes backfire and create tension. Share detailed tips between games so partners have time to absorb them.

Pickleball
DAILY COMPANION

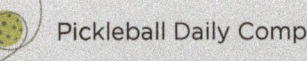

APRIL 20

Build physical adaptability through cross-training. Activities like tai chi, dance, and yoga improve your body's ability to adjust balance and movement patterns quickly during play.

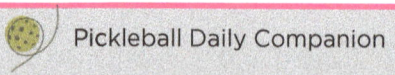
Pickleball Daily Companion

Pickleball
DAILY COMPANION

APRIL 21

Practice hitting from different court positions. Don't just drill from the NVZ line or baseline - practice shots from the transition zone, wide positions, and while moving.

APRIL 22

Wipe down your paddle face after outdoor play, especially after dusty or sandy courts. Clean paddles grip the ball better and last years longer. Check your edge guard for chips that could affect ball contact.

Understand situational shot selection. From the same spot, you might drop, drive, or lob depending on the score, opponents' position, and game momentum. Read the moment and choose accordingly.

Coach's Tip:

Start noticing these subtleties: the drop shot that worked at 5-5 might be the wrong choice at 10-9.

Pickleball
DAILY COMPANION

Pickleball Daily Companion

APRIL 24

Try this approach with bangers: make it a game to see how many of their drives you can turn into soft dinks - transform the challenge into fun practice.

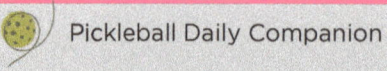

APRIL 25

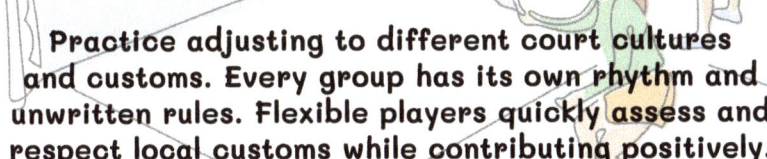

Practice adjusting to different court cultures and customs. Every group has its own rhythm and unwritten rules. Flexible players quickly assess and respect local customs while contributing positively.

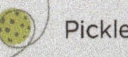

APRIL 26

Build resilience through progressive challenges. Gradually expose yourself to more difficult conditions, opponents, and situations. Physical, mental, and strategic resilience develop through manageable progression.

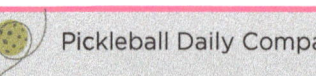

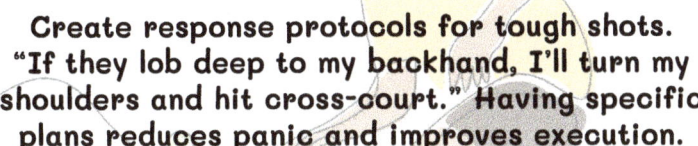

Create response protocols for tough shots.
"If they lob deep to my backhand, I'll turn my
shoulders and hit cross-court." Having specific
plans reduces panic and improves execution.

Pickleball
DAILY COMPANION

Pickleball Daily Companion

APRIL 28

Try "stacking" on the serve when one player is left-handed or has a dominant eye preference. Start both players on the same side, then switch to preferred positions after the serve. This helps partners get to their strongest sides quickly.

Coach's Tip:

Practice these timing patterns with regular partners. The non-server moves to center, then both slide to preferred sides as the ball crosses the net.

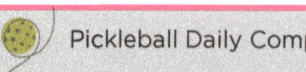

Pickleball Daily Companion

APRIL 29

Players who drill regularly improve much faster than those who only play matches. Drills let you repeat movements until they feel natural, work on weaknesses without pressure, and build muscle memory that shows up when you need it most.

Pickleball
DAILY COMPANION

Pickleball Daily Companion

APRIL 30

Practice one new adaptability skill for 5 minutes before playing today. Whether it's returning to ready position, reading spin, or staying calm under pressure - focused practice builds flexible habits.

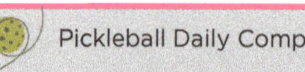

Pickleball Daily Companion

MAY

Discover the art of doubles teamwork and NVZ play. Learn to move as one unit with any partner, communicate effectively under pressure, and dominate the net through smart positioning and patient shot selection. Great partnerships make the game twice as enjoyable.

MAY 1

Read your partner's communication cues beyond just words. Watch for micro hesitations before shots, paddle position changes, or subtle footwork shifts. These signals help you anticipate their needs and adjust your support.

"

Coach's Tip:

Every point is a conversation between four players. Make sure you're speaking the same language as your partner.

 Pickleball Daily Companion

MAY 2

Position yourself right at the non-volley zone line (without touching it). This maximizes your reach and puts you in the best spot to cut off dinks or volleys quickly. The closer you are, the more control you'll have over the pace of play.

Pickleball
DAILY COMPANION

Develop complementary positioning patterns. When your partner moves forward, synchronize with them. When they cover the line, you take the middle. Fluid positioning requires constant micro-adjustments.

MAY 4

In NVZ dinking rallies, aim for the opponent's feet or the area just in front of them. This forces a low, awkward contact point that prevents attacks and often produces pop-ups you can finish.

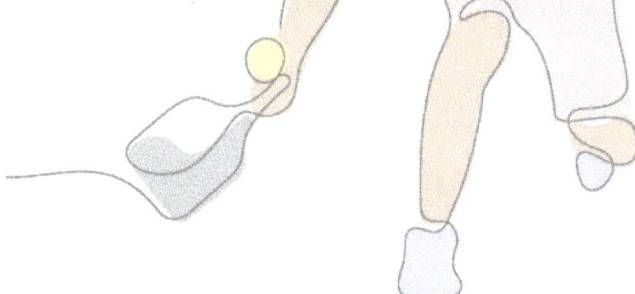

MAY 5

Develop a reset phrase for tense partnership moments. Instead of dwelling on mistakes, use a consistent phrase like "next point focus" to quickly redirect your team's energy forward.

Coach's Tip:

When you stay calm under pressure, you give your partner permission to take smart risks and play their best game.

 Pickleball Daily Companion

MAY 6

Gently redirect the ball at the NVZ line. When opponents speed up the ball, use relaxed wrists and minimal paddle movement to absorb their pace and guide it softly back to their feet. Less swing, more finesse.

 Pickleball Daily Companion

MAY 7

Learn the art of constructive mid-game adjustments. Address strategy changes between points, not during play. Use positive framing: "Let's try hitting more to their backhand" rather than "Stop hitting to their forehand."

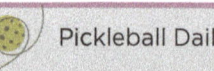

MAY 8

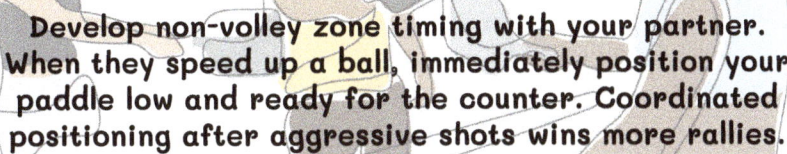

Develop non-volley zone timing with your partner.
When they speed up a ball, immediately position your
paddle low and ready for the counter. Coordinated
positioning after aggressive shots wins more rallies.

MAY 9

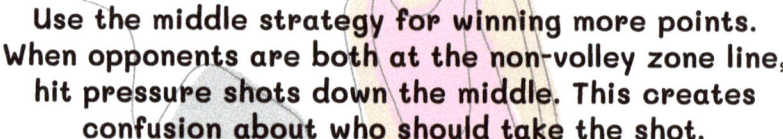

Use the middle strategy for winning more points.
When opponents are both at the non-volley zone line,
hit pressure shots down the middle. This creates
confusion about who should take the shot.

"

Coach's Tip:

Hit down the middle on important points - when serving at 10-9 or returning serve when
behind. When pressure is highest, make opponents communicate.

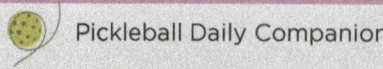

Pickleball Daily Companion

Pickleball
DAILY COMPANION

MAY 10

Learn to recognize speed-up opportunities at the NVZ. When opponents hit a ball above net height, that's your chance to attack - but consider waiting until you've hit 3-4 patient placement shots to set it up. Rushed attacks from the first high ball often sail long.

MAY 11

Maintain correct non-volley zone spacing between you and your partner - about two ball-widths between your paddles when extended. This positioning eliminates the middle gap that opponents love to target.

Coach's Tip:

Make eye contact with your partner between points. This nonverbal connection reinforces teamwork and keeps you both mentally engaged.

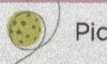 Pickleball Daily Companion

 Pickleball
DAILY COMPANION

MAY 12

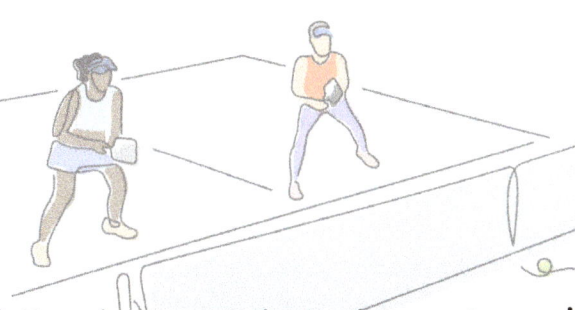

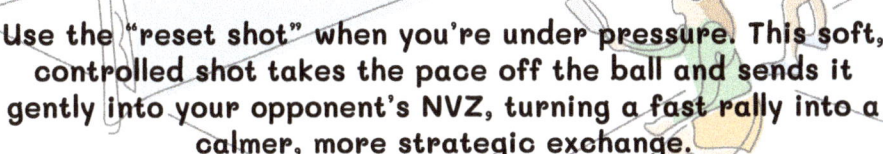

Use the "reset shot" when you're under pressure. This soft, controlled shot takes the pace off the ball and sends it gently into your opponent's NVZ, turning a fast rally into a calmer, more strategic exchange.

Coach's Tip:

Practice your reset shot from difficult positions. When you're stretched or off balance, focus on simply getting the ball up and over the net softly to neutralize the point.

Pickleball
DAILY COMPANION

MAY 13

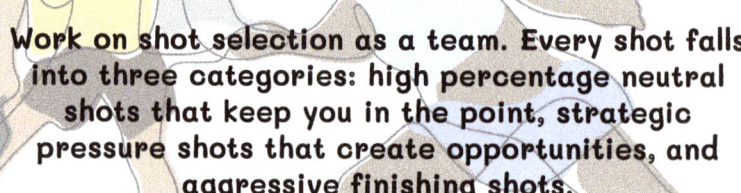

Work on shot selection as a team. Every shot falls into three categories: high percentage neutral shots that keep you in the point, strategic pressure shots that create opportunities, and aggressive finishing shots.

MAY 14

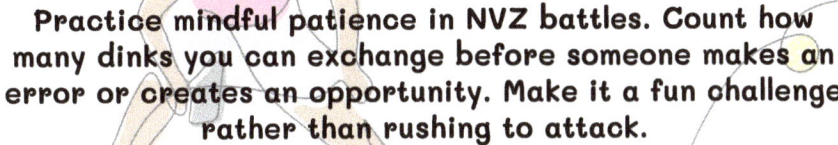

Practice mindful patience in NVZ battles. Count how many dinks you can exchange before someone makes an error or creates an opportunity. Make it a fun challenge rather than rushing to attack.

MAY 15

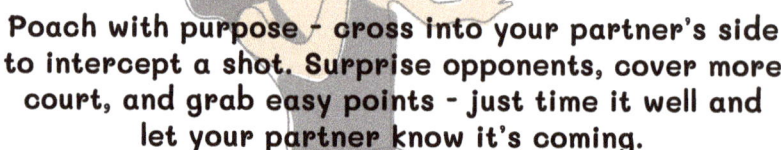

Poach with purpose - cross into your partner's side to intercept a shot. Surprise opponents, cover more court, and grab easy points - just time it well and let your partner know it's coming.

Coach's Tip:

Time your poaches for balls that are within fairly easy reach. The key to elevated play is patience - wait for the right ball.

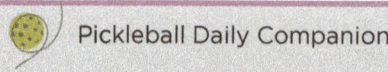

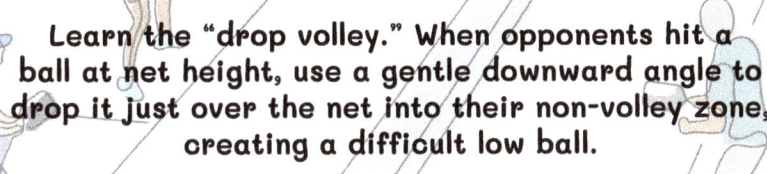

Learn the "drop volley." When opponents hit a ball at net height, use a gentle downward angle to drop it just over the net into their non-volley zone, creating a difficult low ball.

MAY 17

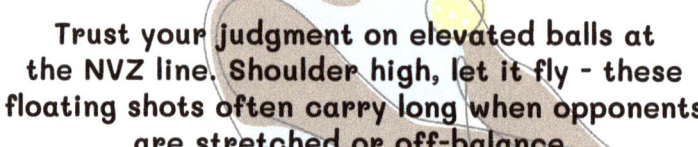

Trust your judgment on elevated balls at the NVZ line. Shoulder high, let it fly - these floating shots often carry long when opponents are stretched or off-balance.

Coach's Tip:

Watch for opponents hitting on the run - they're likely to send it long. And remember that when you're the one scrambling, control beats power every time.

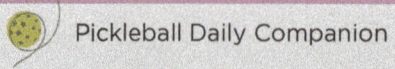

For extremely low shots at the NVZ line, keep your paddle face slightly open and get your paddle head below your wrist level. Use a gentle lifting motion to scoop the ball up and over the net.

Coach's Tip:

Soft hands and minimal swing work better than trying to muscle low balls.

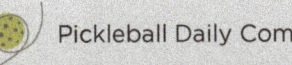
Pickleball Daily Companion

MAY 19

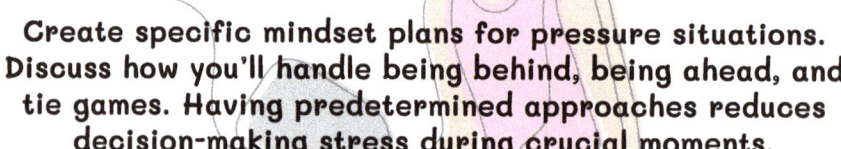

Create specific mindset plans for pressure situations. Discuss how you'll handle being behind, being ahead, and tie games. Having predetermined approaches reduces decision-making stress during crucial moments.

Coach's Tip:

Partnership is about finding someone willing to grow with you, even if it's just for one game.

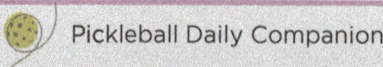

Pickleball Daily Companion

Pickleball
DAILY COMPANION

MAY 20

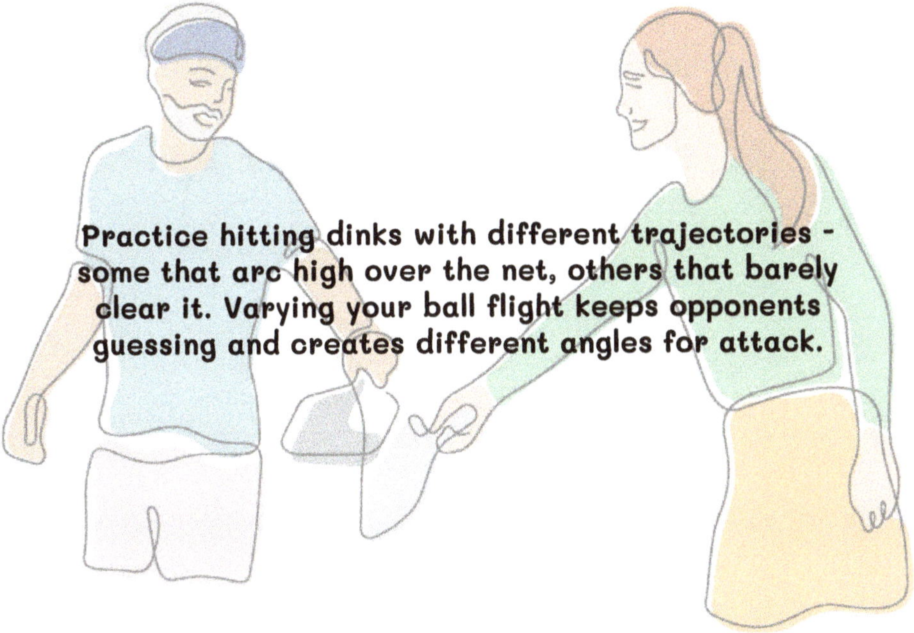

Practice hitting dinks with different trajectories - some that arc high over the net, others that barely clear it. Varying your ball flight keeps opponents guessing and creates different angles for attack.

Pickleball
DAILY COMPANION

MAY 21

When rotating partners frequently, focus on being the steady, encouraging teammate everyone wants to play with again. Consistent positive energy, reliable shot selection, and supportive communication make you a sought-after partner regardless of skill differences.

 Pickleball Daily Companion

MAY 22

Create middle opportunities by hitting your first dink wide to pull one opponent out of position. As they move to cover the corner, the middle opens up for your next shot. This one-two sequence turns patient dinking into aggressive finishing.

 Pickleball Daily Companion

MAY 23

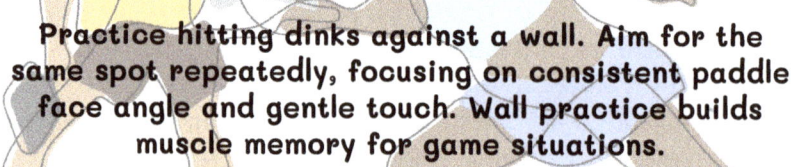

Practice hitting dinks against a wall. Aim for the same spot repeatedly, focusing on consistent paddle face angle and gentle touch. Wall practice builds muscle memory for game situations.

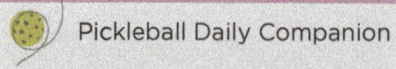

MAY 24

Learn to quickly assess new partners' playing styles. In your first few points together, notice if they prefer aggressive net play or patient baseline rallies, favor forehand or backhand sides, and communicate loudly or quietly. Adapting smoothly to different personalities and skills makes every game more enjoyable.

Pickleball
DAILY COMPANION

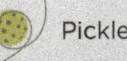 Pickleball Daily Companion

MAY 25

After the serve sequence ends, remember the middle line disappears - either player can cover any ball. When you can't see your partner in your peripheral vision, that's your cue to cover the open space.

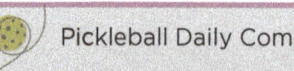

MAY 26

Learn to disguise your NVZ shots. Use the same paddle preparation for drops and speed-ups so opponents can't read your intentions until the ball leaves your paddle.

Practice your shuffle steps at the non-volley zone line. When a ball goes to your partner's side, but they can't reach it, use a quick shuffle step to cover while calling "mine" loudly.

MAY 28

Practice the third shot drop to NVZ corners during warm-up or drills. Aim for where the sideline meets the NVZ line - this placement creates maximum difficulty for opponents while giving you good margin for error.

MAY 29

Call 'no!' instead of 'out!' for balls heading out of bounds. This prevents confusion – your partner won't think you're calling their shot out, and opponents clearly understand you're letting the ball go. The word 'no' is unambiguous and keeps play flowing smoothly.

Pickleball
DAILY COMPANION

MAY 30

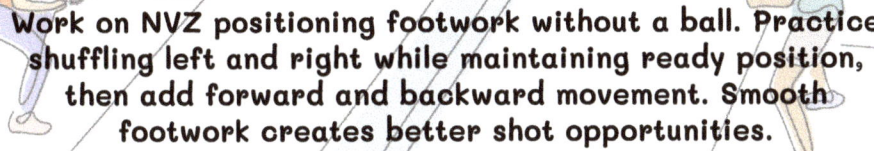

Work on NVZ positioning footwork without a ball. Practice shuffling left and right while maintaining ready position, then add forward and backward movement. Smooth footwork creates better shot opportunities.

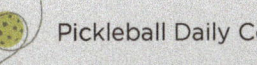

Use partner rotation as a learning laboratory. Each new teammate reveals something about your own game - how you communicate under pressure, adapt to different playing styles, or handle varying skill levels. Every partnership teaches you something new.

JUNE

Think like a strategist. Every shot is a choice - learn to make the right one at the right time. This month covers percentage play, reading opponents, and developing the tactical awareness that separates smart players from lucky ones.

JUNE 1

Learn to read opponent positioning before they even hit. Where they stand and how they prepare reveals their likely shot selection. Position yourself accordingly to get an early advantage.

 Pickleball Daily Companion

JUNE 2

Use "traffic lights" for shot selection based on ball height. Green light (above net) means attack. Yellow light (shoulder-high) means proceed with caution - these balls might be sailing out, so consider letting them go. Red light (below net) means stay patient and keep the rally going.

"

Coach's Tip:

Don't attack from below the net - wait for your green light.

Pickleball
DAILY COMPANION

Pickleball Daily Companion

JUNE 3

Try waiting a few seconds before attacking.
When you see a high ball, pause before
deciding to speed up. This pause prevents
rushing into low percentage attacks.

 Pickleball Daily Companion

JUNE 4

Cross-court shots are high-percentage plays with better success rates than down-the-line shots due to extra distance and lower net height in the middle. When points matter most, choose the diagonal option for reliability over risk.

JUNE 5

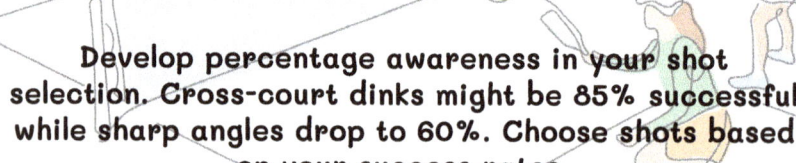

Develop percentage awareness in your shot selection. Cross-court dinks might be 85% successful while sharp angles drop to 60%. Choose shots based on your success rates.

 Pickleball Daily Companion

JUNE 6

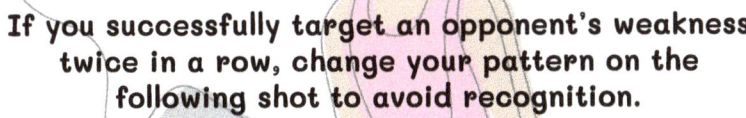

If you successfully target an opponent's weakness twice in a row, change your pattern on the following shot to avoid recognition.

JUNE 7

Resist the urge to end points quickly. Let opponents make mistakes while you play steady, reliable shots. Develop the mindset that patience pays.

Coach's Tip:

Every point you don't give away is a point earned. Smart shot selection means choosing reliability over spectacular attempts most of the time.

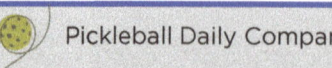 Pickleball Daily Companion

Pickleball
DAILY COMPANION

JUNE 8

Notice when opponents start rushing their shots. This often happens when they're behind or frustrated. Stay calm and give them opportunities to make errors.

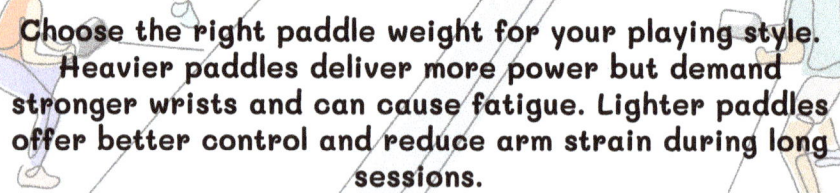

Choose the right paddle weight for your playing style. Heavier paddles deliver more power but demand stronger wrists and can cause fatigue. Lighter paddles offer better control and reduce arm strain during long sessions.

JUNE 10

Tune into how long the ball stays on your paddle - known as "dwell time." When the ball stays on your paddle a moment longer, you gain control and spin for precise shots like dinks and drops. For faster, more powerful shots, use a quicker release (less dwell time). Practicing this awareness trains your feel for the ball, improving your shot selection and timing.

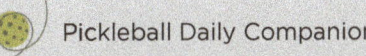

Consider giving the opposing team a "gift" as part of your own strategy. Send over a slightly higher ball to attack, then be ready with your paddle in defensive position for their predictable downward return.

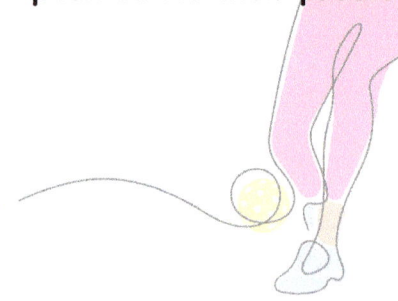

JUNE 12

Next time you're on court, notice players who keep shifting their grip or bouncing in place - it often means they're overthinking. Stay calm and focused to play your best.

"

Coach's Tip:

Smart players collect information about opponents throughout the match. Mental notes about their patterns become your strategic advantage.

Pickleball
DAILY COMPANION

Pickleball Daily Companion

JUNE 13

Develop your third shot selection based on opponent positioning. If they're both back, drop short. If one is up and one back, drive to the back player. Match your shots to their court position.

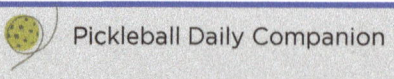

JUNE 14

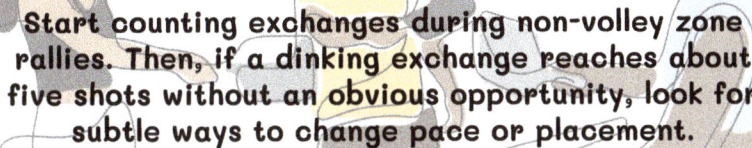

Start counting exchanges during non-volley zone rallies. Then, if a dinking exchange reaches about five shots without an obvious opportunity, look for subtle ways to change pace or placement.

JUNE 15

Learn to "sell" the wrong shot with your body language. Look cross-court but hit down the line. Point your shoulders one way but go the other. Deception creates openings.

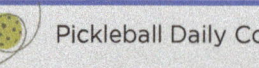

Pickleball Daily Companion

JUNE 16

Develop shot selection based on your energy level. When fresh, take more aggressive positions and shots. When tired, focus on placement and percentage play.

Pickleball
DAILY COMPANION

Pickleball Daily Companion

JUNE 17

Don't always attack the first high ball - wait for opponents to hit 2-3 shots that truly set up your opportunity. Patient players create better chances than aggressive ones.

JUNE 18

Learn to read the "point rhythm." Fast, chaotic points need simple shot choices. Slow, building rallies allow for more complex strategic planning and execution.

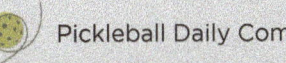

JUNE 19

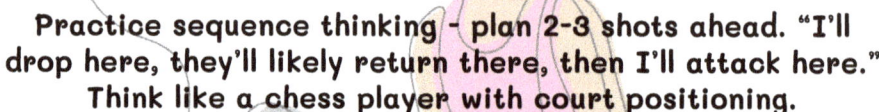

Practice sequence thinking - plan 2-3 shots ahead. "I'll drop here, they'll likely return there, then I'll attack here." Think like a chess player with court positioning.

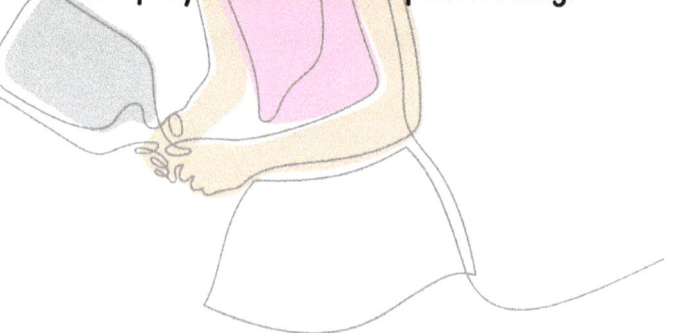

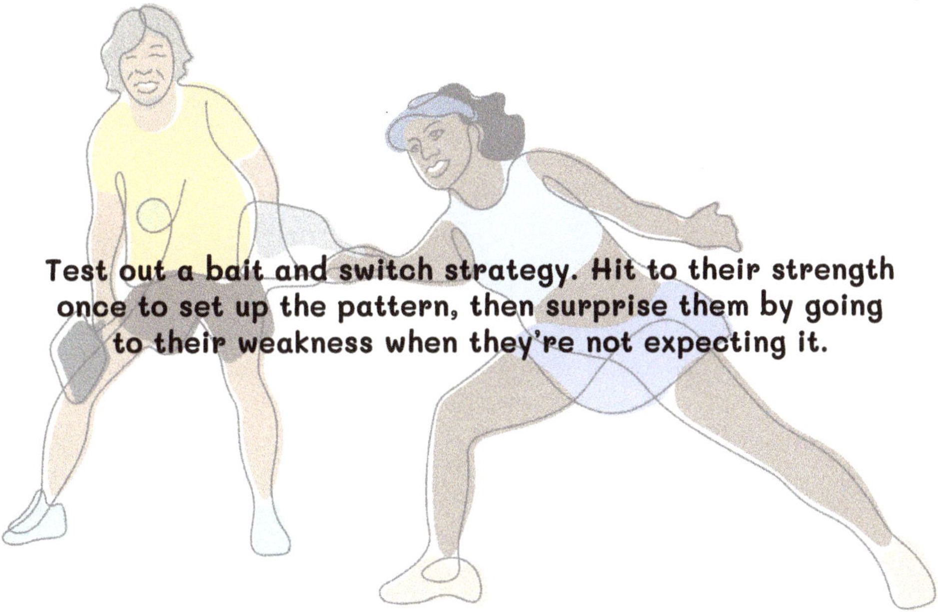

Test out a bait and switch strategy. Hit to their strength once to set up the pattern, then surprise them by going to their weakness when they're not expecting it.

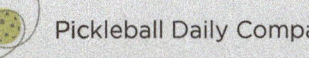

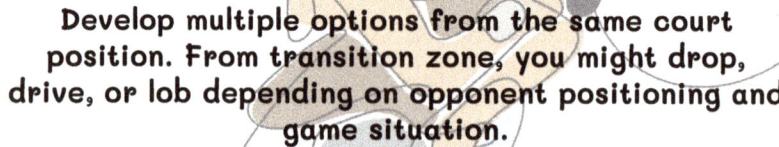

Develop multiple options from the same court position. From transition zone, you might drop, drive, or lob depending on opponent positioning and game situation.

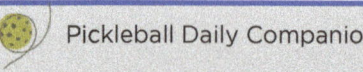

Pickleball Daily Companion

Pickleball
DAILY COMPANION

JUNE 22

Try this approach when points feel intense: hit one intentionally slower shot to release tension and reset the rally rhythm.

Pickleball
DAILY COMPANION

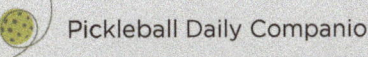

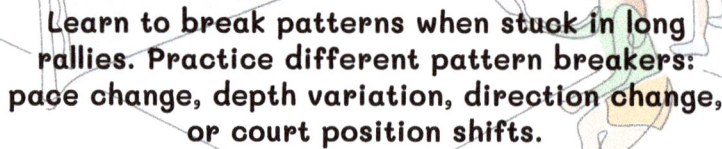

Learn to break patterns when stuck in long rallies. Practice different pattern breakers: pace change, depth variation, direction change, or court position shifts.

JUNE 24

Spot the "lean tells" in opponents. When they lean left, they're often preparing to move or hit left. Use this body language to anticipate their next move.

 Pickleball Daily Companion

JUNE 25

Choose shots that give your team the best advantage for the next exchange. Think of each shot as setting up your partnership for success, not just ending points.

Coach's Tip:
When you know a shot usually works, you execute it with less tension and doubt. Confidence in shot selection improves execution.

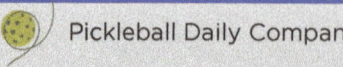
Pickleball Daily Companion

Pickleball
DAILY COMPANION

JUNE 26

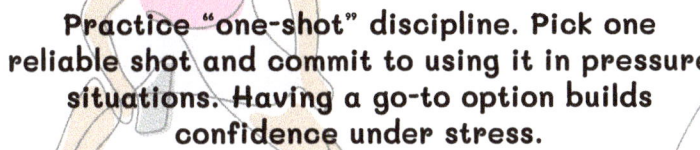

Practice "one-shot" discipline. Pick one reliable shot and commit to using it in pressure situations. Having a go-to option builds confidence under stress.

Pickleball
DAILY COMPANION

Pickleball Daily Companion

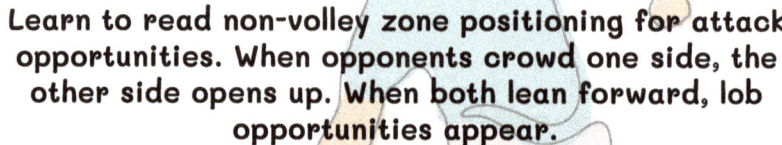

Learn to read non-volley zone positioning for attack opportunities. When opponents crowd one side, the other side opens up. When both lean forward, lob opportunities appear.

 Pickleball Daily Companion

JUNE 28

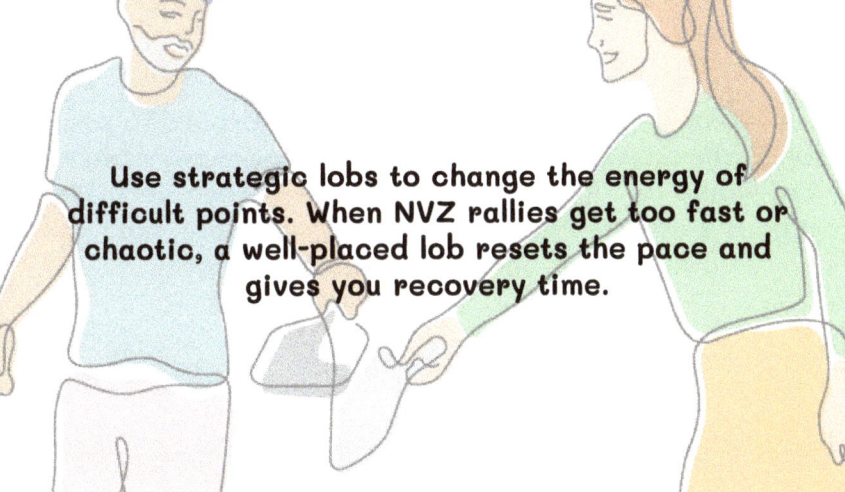

Use strategic lobs to change the energy of difficult points. When NVZ rallies get too fast or chaotic, a well-placed lob resets the pace and gives you recovery time.

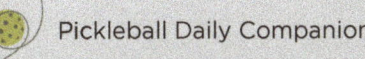

JUNE 29

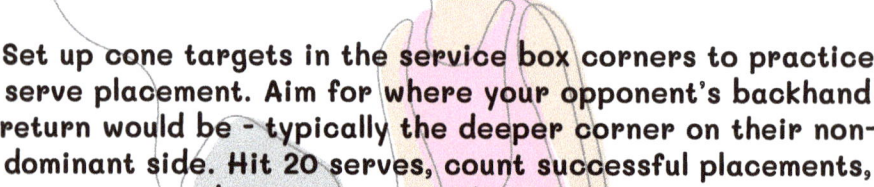

Set up cone targets in the service box corners to practice serve placement. Aim for where your opponent's backhand return would be - typically the deeper corner on their non-dominant side. Hit 20 serves, count successful placements, and track your weekly improvement.

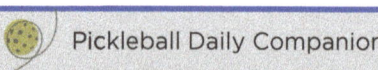

JUNE 30

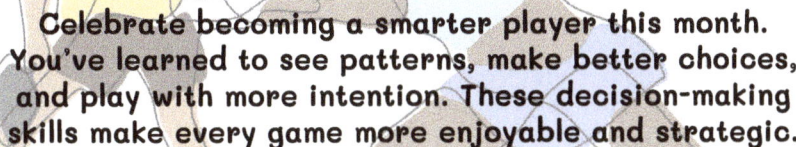

Celebrate becoming a smarter player this month.
You've learned to see patterns, make better choices,
and play with more intention. These decision-making
skills make every game more enjoyable and strategic.

Coach's Tip:

Take one insight from this month into your next game and watch how it
changes everything.

JULY

 HEALTH & WELLNESS

Your body is your most important piece of equipment. Focus on injury prevention, energy management, proper biomechanics, and the joy of movement. When you feel strong and healthy, every game becomes more fun and sustainable.

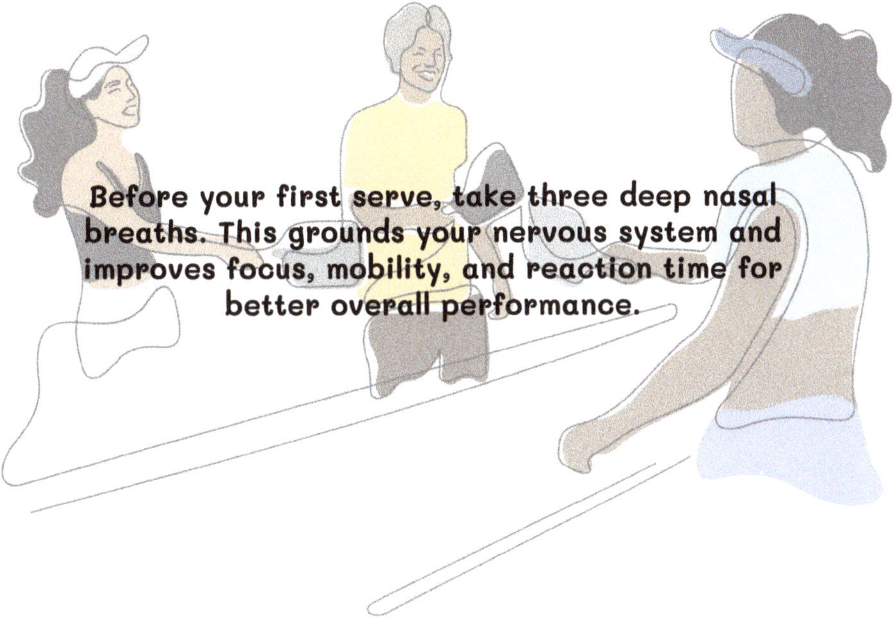

Before your first serve, take three deep nasal breaths. This grounds your nervous system and improves focus, mobility, and reaction time for better overall performance.

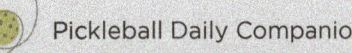

JULY 2

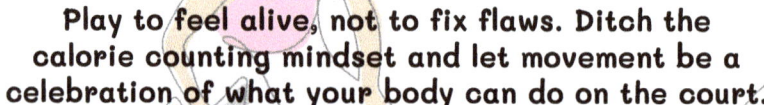

Play to feel alive, not to fix flaws. Ditch the calorie counting mindset and let movement be a celebration of what your body can do on the court.

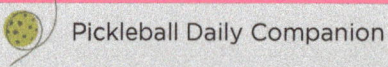
Pickleball Daily Companion

Pickleball
DAILY COMPANION

JULY 3

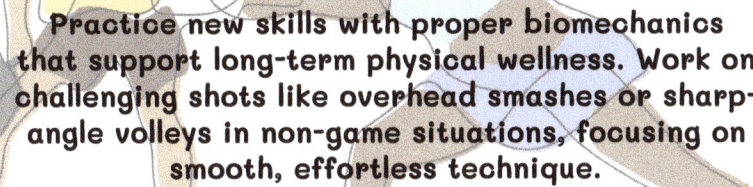

Practice new skills with proper biomechanics that support long-term physical wellness. Work on challenging shots like overhead smashes or sharp-angle volleys in non-game situations, focusing on smooth, effortless technique.

Pickleball
DAILY COMPANION

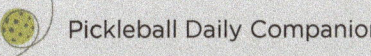

JULY 4

Use your pre-serve routine to activate your parasympathetic nervous system. Two bounces plus a slow exhale lowers cortisol and improves focus naturally.

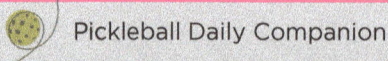

JULY 5

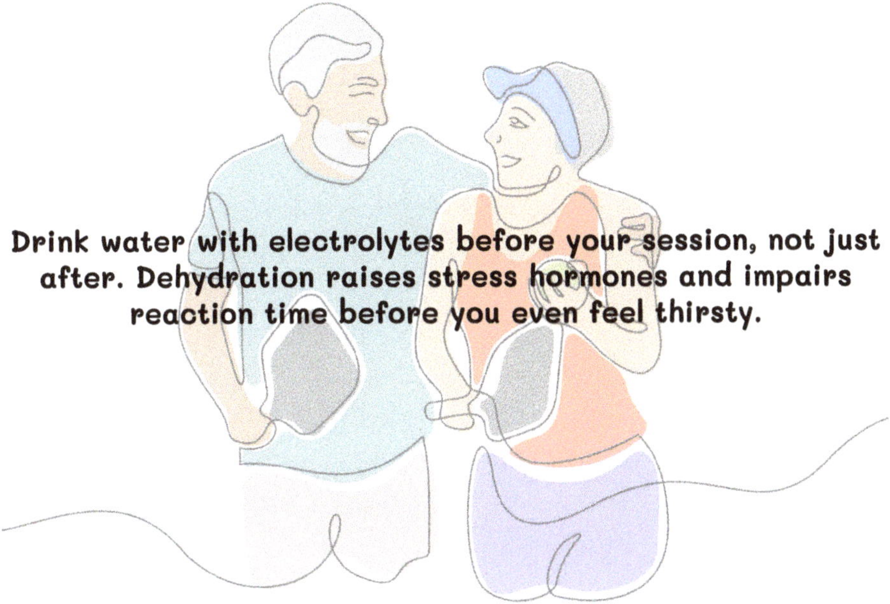

Drink water with electrolytes before your session, not just after. Dehydration raises stress hormones and impairs reaction time before you even feel thirsty.

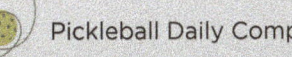

JULY 6

Stretch your chest and shoulders before playing. Better posture equals better breathing, improved shot control, and a more positive mindset on court.

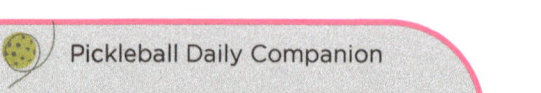

Pickleball Daily Companion

Pickleball
DAILY COMPANION

JULY 7

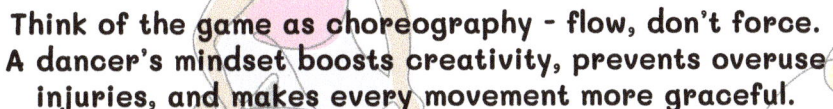

Think of the game as choreography – flow, don't force.
A dancer's mindset boosts creativity, prevents overuse
injuries, and makes every movement more graceful.

JULY 8

Scan your feet before each serve. Are they tense or grounded? Where tension lives in your foundation, injury often follows. Awareness prevents problems.

Coach's Tip:

Notice how energy transfers from your big toe through the ball of your foot, to your heel, then up through your knee and hip. This kinetic chain is the foundation of safe, sustainable play.

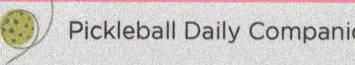

JULY 9

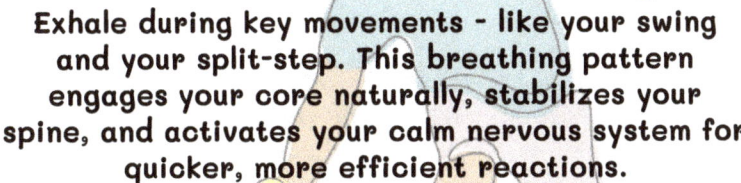

Exhale during key movements - like your swing and your split-step. This breathing pattern engages your core naturally, stabilizes your spine, and activates your calm nervous system for quicker, more efficient reactions.

Pickleball
DAILY COMPANION

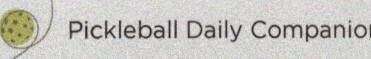

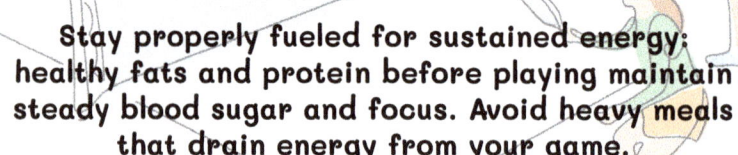

Stay properly fueled for sustained energy:
healthy fats and protein before playing maintain
steady blood sugar and focus. Avoid heavy meals
that drain energy from your game.

JULY 11

For every hard drive you hit, add a drop or dink.
Balanced gameplay supports joint longevity and
keeps your mental approach flexible and strategic.

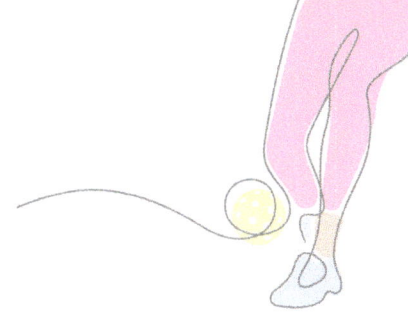

Pickleball
DAILY COMPANION

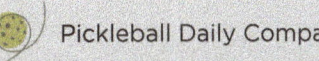
Pickleball Daily Companion

JULY 12

Use humor as recovery - a well-timed joke mid-match boosts feel-good hormones and rewires perfectionist thinking.

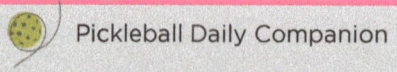
Pickleball Daily Companion

JULY 13

Respect your energy edge - fatigue signals feedback not failure. Stop one game early when needed. Strategic recovery is part of peak performance, not weakness.

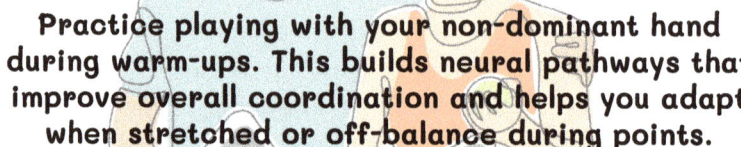

Practice playing with your non-dominant hand during warm-ups. This builds neural pathways that improve overall coordination and helps you adapt when stretched or off-balance during points.

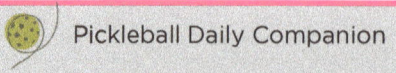

Pickleball
DAILY COMPANION

Sit for 60 seconds with eyes closed after playing. Let your body integrate the movement patterns and experiences. Mental recovery matters as much as physical recovery.

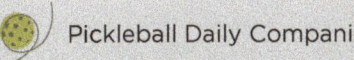

JULY 16

Practice light foot drills barefoot at home. This strengthens stabilizing muscles, prevents ankle injuries, and improves your body's spatial awareness on court.

Coach's Tip:

Your feet contain thousands of nerve endings. Training them barefoot awakens sensors that improve your balance and movement quality.

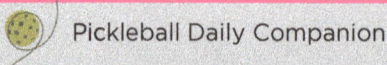

Pickleball Daily Companion

Pickleball
DAILY COMPANION

JULY 17

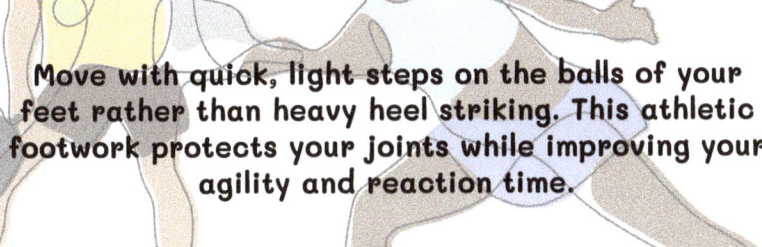

Move with quick, light steps on the balls of your feet rather than heavy heel striking. This athletic footwork protects your joints while improving your agility and reaction time.

Pickleball
DAILY COMPANION

JULY 18

Choose outdoor courts, when possible, for natural Vitamin D and fresh air. Humans evolved to spend time outside, but most of us live indoors almost 24 hours of the day. Pickleball gives you the perfect excuse to soak up sunlight, breathe fresh air and connect with nature.

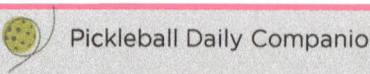

JULY 19

Use your whole body for power, not just your arm. Tennis elbow often develops when players try to muscle shots instead of using proper rotation and weight transfer.

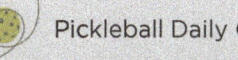

JULY 20

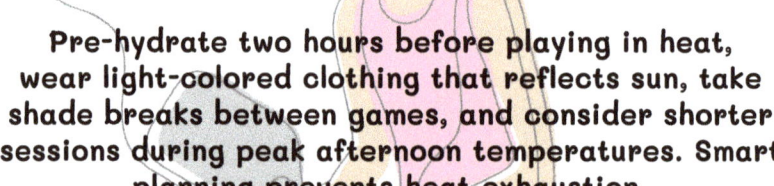

Pre-hydrate two hours before playing in heat, wear light-colored clothing that reflects sun, take shade breaks between games, and consider shorter sessions during peak afternoon temperatures. Smart planning prevents heat exhaustion.

JULY 21

Pick one body area - shoulders, grip, forehead - and consciously soften it. Tension drains power, speed, and enjoyment from your game.

Coach's Tip:

Mid-match, scan your jaw for tension. If it's clenched, so is your swing. Release facial tension and watch your whole body soften and flow better.

Pickleball
DAILY COMPANION

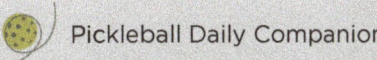
Pickleball Daily Companion

JULY 22

Never go backwards to retrieve a lob - always turn and shuffle sideways or run. Backpedaling is unstable and dangerous. Pivot, turn, and move forward safely to the ball.

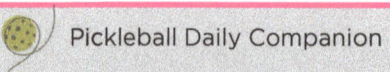

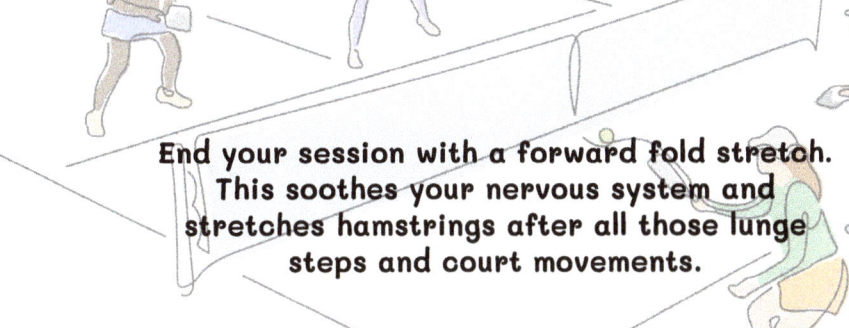

End your session with a forward fold stretch. This soothes your nervous system and stretches hamstrings after all those lunge steps and court movements.

Pickleball
DAILY COMPANION

JULY 24

Ground your bare feet in grass or sand after playing. This natural grounding reduces inflammation in your body and helps recalibrate your nervous system.

Bend your knees, not your back, when hitting low balls. This protects your spine while giving you better paddle control. Athletic position starts with your legs doing the work.

Pickleball
DAILY COMPANION

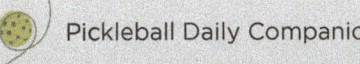

JULY 26

Hold each stretch in your warm-up and cool-down for at least 30 seconds with intention. Let your body feel heard and cared for, not rushed through a mechanical routine.

Pickleball Daily Companion

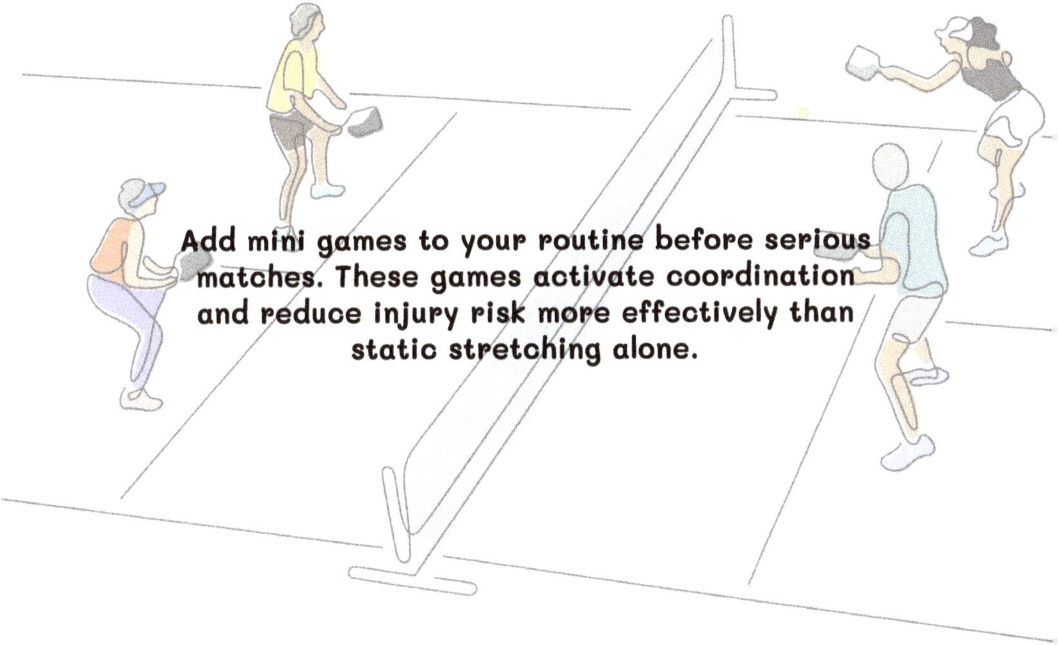

Add mini games to your routine before serious matches. These games activate coordination and reduce injury risk more effectively than static stretching alone.

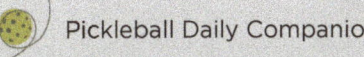

JULY 28

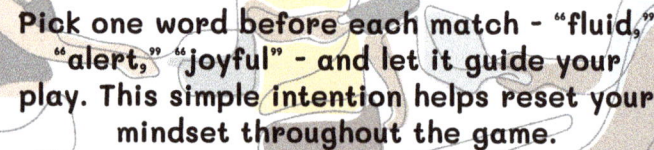

Pick one word before each match - "fluid," "alert," "joyful" - and let it guide your play. This simple intention helps reset your mindset throughout the game.

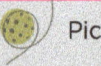 Pickleball Daily Companion

When you make mistakes, ask: "Did I learn, adjust, or just repeat?" This mental clarity turns errors into upgrades rather than sources of frustration.

Treat sweating as therapeutic detox. Your skin is a major detox organ - embrace the purge and appreciate your body's natural cooling and cleansing process.

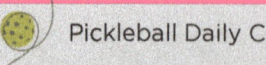

Pickleball
DAILY COMPANION

JULY 31

End each session by thanking your body: "Thank you knees, thank you breath." This reinforces self-respect and deepens your mind-body connection for lasting wellness.

Coach's Tip:

Gratitude to your body creates a positive feedback loop that enhances both performance and enjoyment on court.

Pickleball
DAILY COMPANION

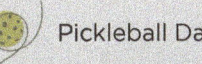

Pickleball Daily Companion

AUGUST

Control the start of every point. Develop serves that create immediate advantages and returns that seize control from your opponents. These opening shots set the tone for everything that follows, so make them count.

Pickleball Daily Companion

Pickleball
DAILY COMPANION

AUGUST 1

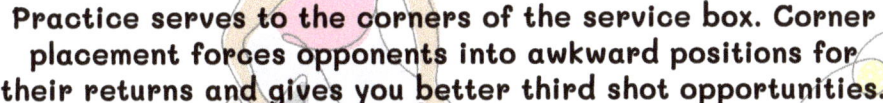

Practice serves to the corners of the service box. Corner placement forces opponents into awkward positions for their returns and gives you better third shot opportunities.

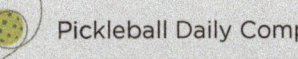

AUGUST 2

Read your opponent's return stance before serving. If they're positioned wide, serve to the opposite corner. If they're crowding the center, aim for the sidelines.

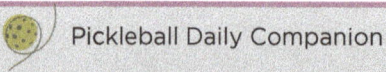

Pickleball Daily Companion

AUGUST 3

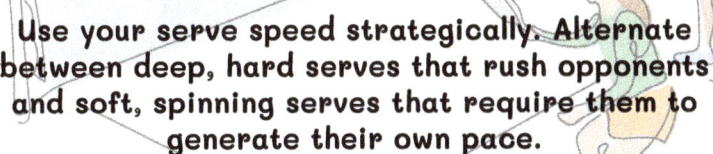

Use your serve speed strategically. Alternate between deep, hard serves that rush opponents and soft, spinning serves that require them to generate their own pace.

AUGUST 4

The non-receiving partner has one job and one job only - watch the serve like a hawk. While your partner focuses on returning, you determine if the serve is in or out. Call it clearly and immediately. This division of responsibility prevents confusion and ensures accurate line calls.

AUGUST 5

Move to the net when returning short serves. When opponents serve shallow, step forward aggressively and attack with pace or sharp angles for immediate pressure.

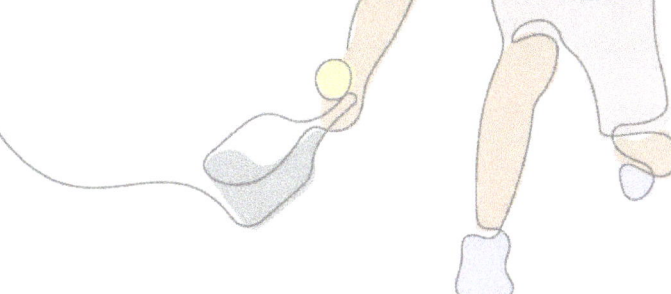

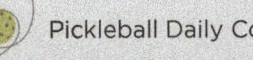

AUGUST 6

Develop serve placement patterns that set up your favorite third shots. If you love drop shots, serve deep to their backhand. If you prefer drives, serve to create weak returns.

Coach's Tip:

Serving starts not only the point - it also starts your strategy. Every serve should have a purpose.

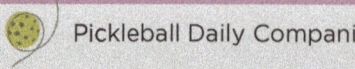
Pickleball Daily Companion

Pickleball
DAILY COMPANION

AUGUST 7

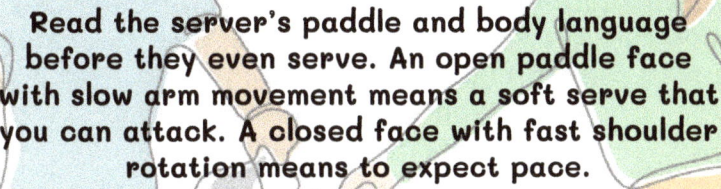

Read the server's paddle and body language before they even serve. An open paddle face with slow arm movement means a soft serve that you can attack. A closed face with fast shoulder rotation means to expect pace.

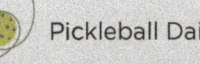

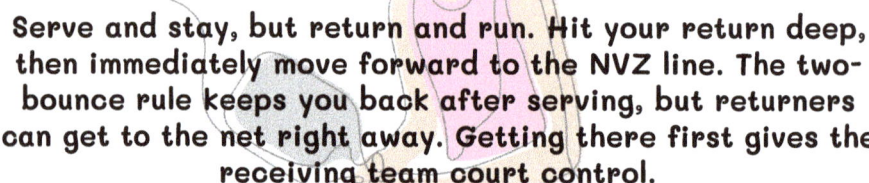

Serve and stay, but return and run. Hit your return deep, then immediately move forward to the NVZ line. The two-bounce rule keeps you back after serving, but returners can get to the net right away. Getting there first gives the receiving team court control.

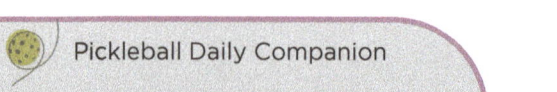

AUGUST 9

Practice returning serves from different court positions. Stay back for hard serves, step forward for soft ones. Positioning yourself based on what's coming creates better contact and shot options.

 Pickleball Daily Companion

AUGUST 10

Serve with intentional spin to create unpredictable bounces. Topspin dips fast after the bounce, slice skids and stays low, sidespin pulls opponents off court.

Coach's Tip:

Your serve should create problems for opponents while setting up solutions for your team.

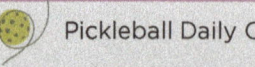
Pickleball Daily Companion

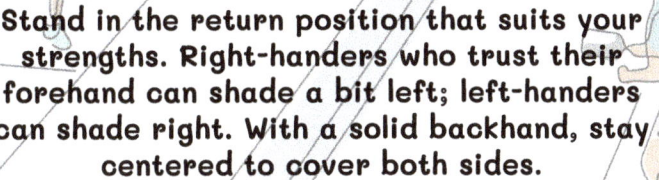

Stand in the return position that suits your strengths. Right-handers who trust their forehand can shade a bit left; left-handers can shade right. With a solid backhand, stay centered to cover both sides.

Coach's Tip:

Developing a dependable backhand gives you more options and keeps opponents from targeting your weaker side.

Pickleball
DAILY COMPANION

 Pickleball Daily Companion

Know when to advance and when to stay back.
After hitting a strong, deep return, move
forward confidently. After weaker returns that
give opponents attacking opportunities, stay
back and prepare to defend.

Return serves to your opponent's feet in the transition zone. This creates awkward half-volleys that often result in weak third shots you can attack.

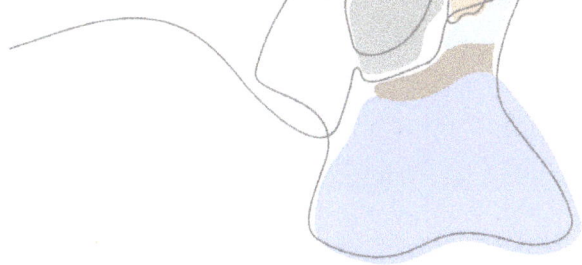

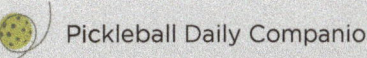

AUGUST 14

Practice serving under pressure during warm-ups. Aim for specific targets even during practice, not just during games. Pressure practice builds confidence.

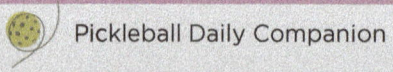

AUGUST 15

Adjust your serve to match the wind. In headwinds, add topspin to drive the ball through. In tailwinds, aim lower and take a little pace off. In crosswinds, use slice to keep shots low. When gusts are unpredictable, aim well inside the sidelines for safety.

AUGUST 16

Use return placement to dictate the rally flow. Return cross-court for longer rallies, down-the-line for quick points, to the middle to create confusion.

Coach's Tip:

Every return is an opportunity to seize control of the point. Don't just get it back - put it somewhere with purpose.

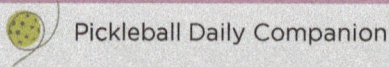

Pickleball Daily Companion

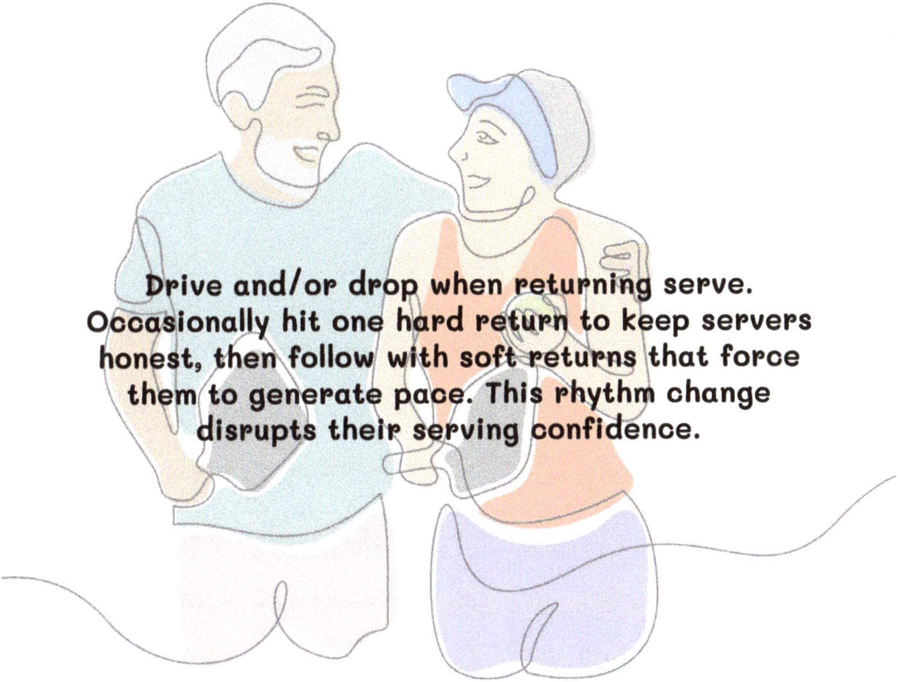

Drive and/or drop when returning serve. Occasionally hit one hard return to keep servers honest, then follow with soft returns that force them to generate pace. This rhythm change disrupts their serving confidence.

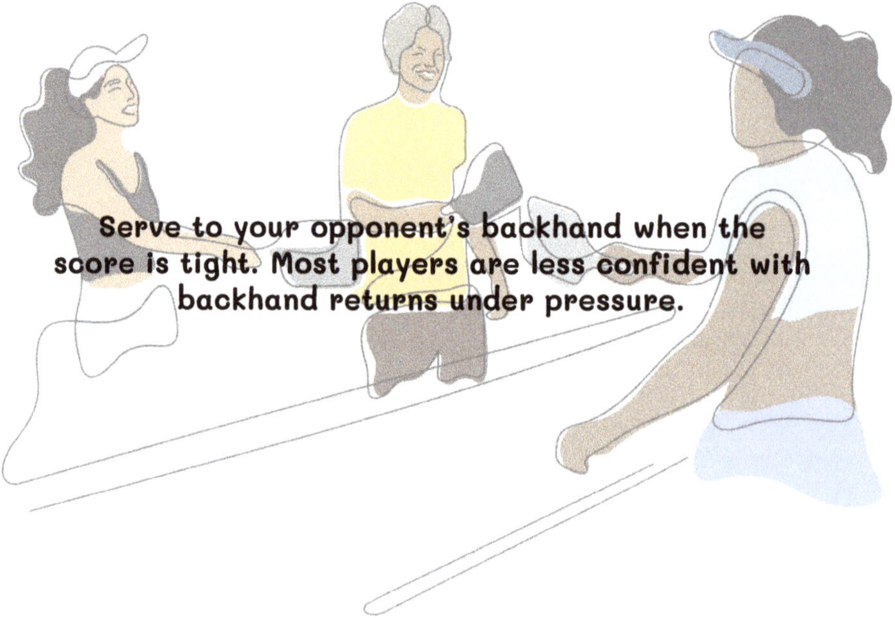

Serve to your opponent's backhand when the score is tight. Most players are less confident with backhand returns under pressure.

Pickleball Daily Companion

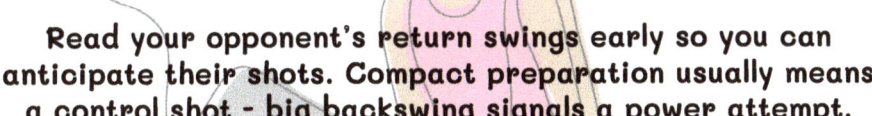

Read your opponent's return swings early so you can anticipate their shots. Compact preparation usually means a control shot - big backswing signals a power attempt.

Pickleball
DAILY COMPANION

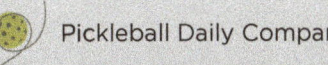
Pickleball Daily Companion

AUGUST 20

Use serving rhythm to your advantage. Vary your pace between serves - sometimes quick, sometimes with extra bounces - to disrupt opponent timing.

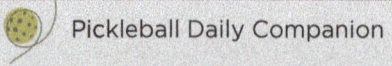

AUGUST 21

Practice returning serves while moving. Many serves require you to adjust your position, so practice hitting quality returns on the move.

Coach's Tip:

The best returners make difficult serves look easy through optimal court positioning and preparation.

AUGUST 22

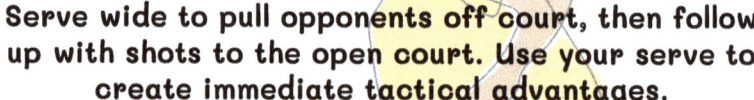

Serve wide to pull opponents off court, then follow up with shots to the open court. Use your serve to create immediate tactical advantages.

Pickleball
DAILY COMPANION

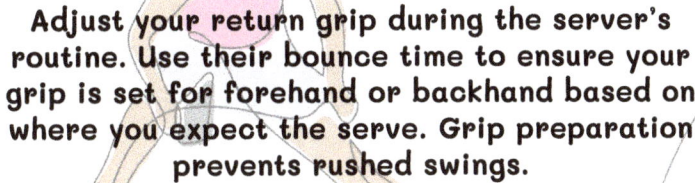

Adjust your return grip during the server's routine. Use their bounce time to ensure your grip is set for forehand or backhand based on where you expect the serve. Grip preparation prevents rushed swings.

Pickleball
DAILY COMPANION

Pickleball Daily Companion

AUGUST 24

Use soft drop serves occasionally to change the pace and force opponents to generate their own power. This disrupts their return rhythm.

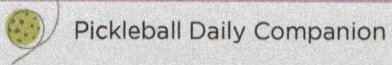

AUGUST 25

Work on returning serves deep to their backhand corner. This forces them into difficult third shots instead of easy attacks. Make their strongest weapon harder to use.

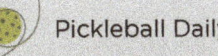

AUGUST 26

Practice serves that land within two feet of the baseline. This depth consistently creates difficult returns and puts immediate pressure on opponents.

Coach's Tip:

Consistency beats power in serving. A reliable, deep serve gives you control of more points than occasional aces.

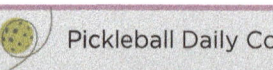 Pickleball Daily Companion

 Pickleball
DAILY COMPANION

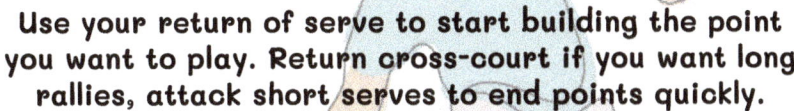

Use your return of serve to start building the point you want to play. Return cross-court if you want long rallies, attack short serves to end points quickly.

Pickleball
DAILY COMPANION

AUGUST 28

Read server positioning before they serve. Servers who stand close to the centerline often serve wide, those positioned wide often serve toward center.

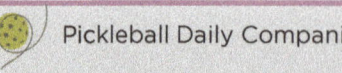

AUGUST 29

Return and reposition instantly. After hitting your return, immediately move toward the net rather than watching the ball or admiring your shot.

AUGUST 30

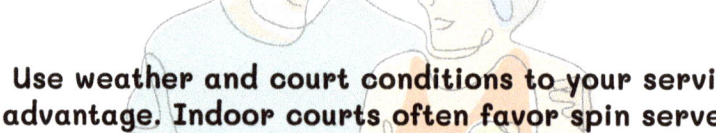

Use weather and court conditions to your serving advantage. Indoor courts often favor spin serves - outdoor wind affects placement choices.

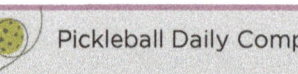

AUGUST 31

Learn return stances for different serve types. Use a closed stance (front foot closer to baseline) for power returns, open stance (front foot closer to net) for placement returns, and neutral stance when unsure. Proper footwork creates better shot opportunities.

Coach's Tip:

Serving and returning well gives you more third and fourth shot opportunities. Control the start of points to control the outcome.

Pickleball
DAILY COMPANION

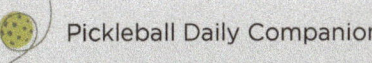
Pickleball Daily Companion

SEPTEMBER

 ADVANCED TECHNIQUES

Ready to add some artistry to your game? Build on your solid fundamentals with more sophisticated shots and creative strategies. These techniques open up new possibilities and give you fresh ways to solve challenging situations on court.

Celebrate how far you've come! This month, discover the joy in more sophisticated shots. Notice techniques that once felt impossible are now within reach. You've built the foundation; now add some artistry.

Pickleball Daily Companion

SEPTEMBER 2

Build advanced techniques from strong fundamentals. Know your grip, stance, footwork, spacing, and timing before adding complexity. Strong basics make everything else easier and more reliable.

SEPTEMBER 3

Communicate before attempting challenging shots. Call "Going wide!" when chasing sharp angles so your partner covers the middle. Advanced shots work beautifully when your partner anticipates your move.

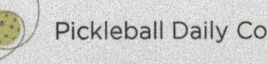

SEPTEMBER 4

Learn NVZ strategy beyond basic dinking. Focus first on consistent smart placement, then add pace and spin changes. Decide which player will be more aggressive while the other provides steady support.

Coach's Tip:
If a NVZ rally provides a ball well above the net, that's your earned opportunity to attack. Before that, your job is patience and precise placement.

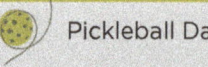 Pickleball Daily Companion

SEPTEMBER 5

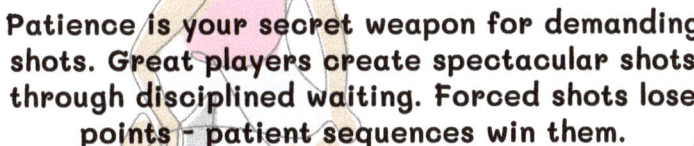

Patience is your secret weapon for demanding shots. Great players create spectacular shots through disciplined waiting. Forced shots lose points - patient sequences win them.

Pickleball
DAILY COMPANION

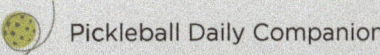

SEPTEMBER 6

Encourage others when they attempt new skills.
A simple "Nice try!" when someone goes for
challenging shots creates supportive environments
where everyone feels safe to experiment.

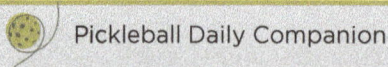

Pickleball Daily Companion

Pickleball
DAILY COMPANION

SEPTEMBER 7

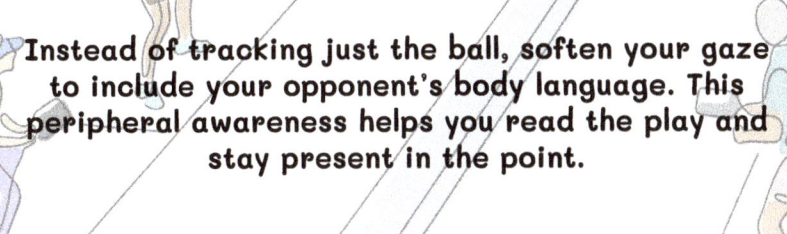

Instead of tracking just the ball, soften your gaze to include your opponent's body language. This peripheral awareness helps you read the play and stay present in the point.

Pickleball
DAILY COMPANION

Pickleball Daily Companion

SEPTEMBER 8

Consider working with a qualified instructor to unlock your next breakthrough. Fresh eyes can spot subtle technical areas that self-teaching often misses.

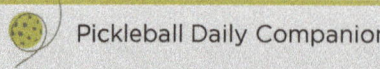

Pickleball Daily Companion

SEPTEMBER 9

Practice third shot drop variations, mixing up trajectories, spins, and placements. Each variation creates new problems for opponents to solve and adds colors to your strategic palette.

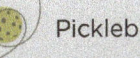

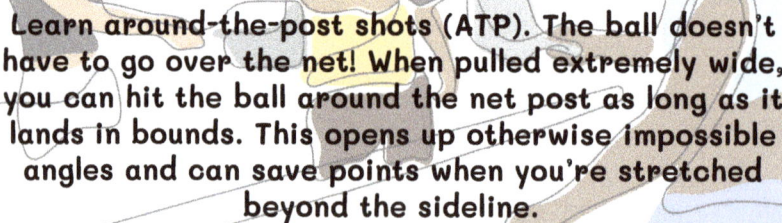

Learn around-the-post shots (ATP). The ball doesn't have to go over the net! When pulled extremely wide, you can hit the ball around the net post as long as it lands in bounds. This opens up otherwise impossible angles and can save points when you're stretched beyond the sideline.

 Pickleball Daily Companion

 Pickleball

SEPTEMBER 11

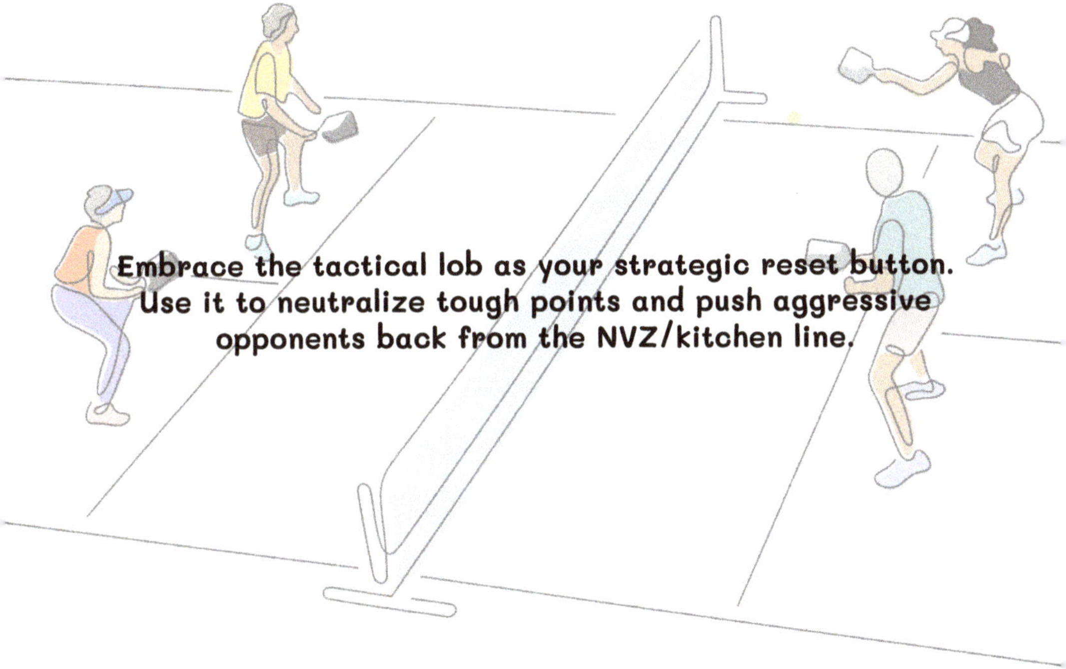

Embrace the tactical lob as your strategic reset button. Use it to neutralize tough points and push aggressive opponents back from the NVZ/kitchen line.

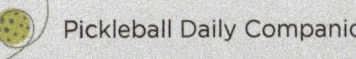

SEPTEMBER 12

Build confidence through positive self-talk and gradual progression. Design practice sequences that gradually increase difficulty while maintaining encouraging internal dialogue.

Coach's Tip:
Start with shots you can make 8 out of 10 times, then gradually add complexity. Success builds on success.

 Pickleball Daily Companion

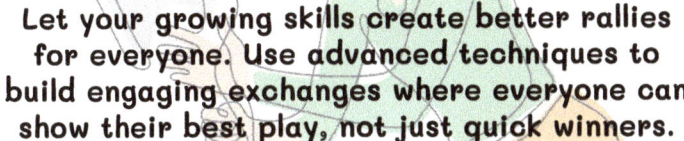

Let your growing skills create better rallies for everyone. Use advanced techniques to build engaging exchanges where everyone can show their best play, not just quick winners.

SEPTEMBER 14

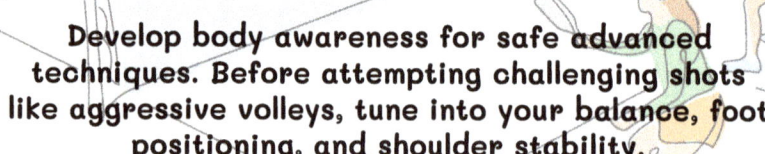

Develop body awareness for safe advanced techniques. Before attempting challenging shots like aggressive volleys, tune into your balance, foot positioning, and shoulder stability.

"

Coach's Tip:

Pickleball draws from the best of dance and martial arts. Movement should be efficient, protective and expressive all at once.

 Pickleball Daily Companion

SEPTEMBER 15

When stretching for low balls - whether dinks or defensive resets - hold your paddle face parallel to the ground, like a pancake, with your palm up. This helps lift them over the net more effectively.

Pickleball
DAILY COMPANION

Pickleball Daily Companion

SEPTEMBER 16

Develop soft hands for slowing down fast balls at the net. Instead of swinging at speed-ups, gently push the ball with relaxed wrists and minimal paddle movement. This absorbs pace and redirects balls softly to opponents' feet.

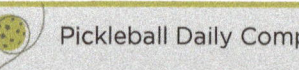

SEPTEMBER 17

Maintain your defensive wall when points get scrambled. Even when pulled out of normal position, keep roughly the same distance from your partner. Two players moving together cover more court than two individuals.

Pickleball
DAILY COMPANION

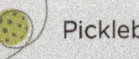

SEPTEMBER 18

Vary your contact point for different spins. Contact the ball early and high for topspin drives, late and low for slice drops. Timing changes create different ball flights from similar positions.

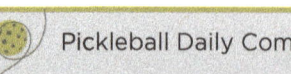

Pickleball Daily Companion

SEPTEMBER 19

Develop the ability to hit quality shots while moving. Practice dinking, driving, and dropping while shuffling left or right. When you can hit solid shots on the move, you'll handle pressure situations with confidence.

Pickleball
DAILY COMPANION

SEPTEMBER 20

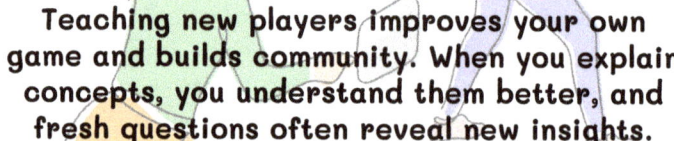

Teaching new players improves your own game and builds community. When you explain concepts, you understand them better, and fresh questions often reveal new insights.

Coach's Tip:
You only need to be one step ahead of who you're helping. A thoughtful 3.0 player teaching a 2.0 player has fresh perspective and remembers recent breakthroughs.

 Pickleball Daily Companion

Work on the art of changing rally rhythm mid-point. Hit three or four shots at one pace, then dramatically slow down or speed up your next shot. Rhythm breaks often force errors or create opportunities.

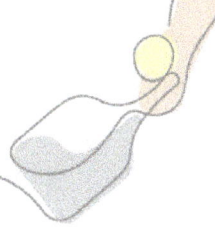
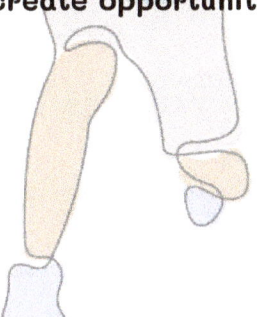

SEPTEMBER 22

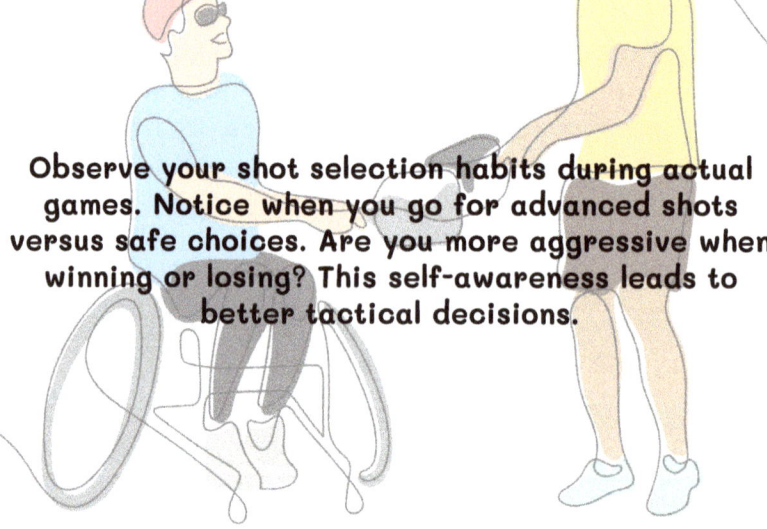

Observe your shot selection habits during actual games. Notice when you go for advanced shots versus safe choices. Are you more aggressive when winning or losing? This self-awareness leads to better tactical decisions.

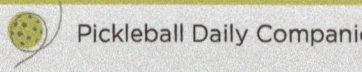

SEPTEMBER 23

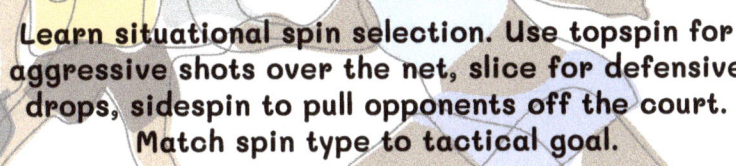

Learn situational spin selection. Use topspin for aggressive shots over the net, slice for defensive drops, sidespin to pull opponents off the court. Match spin type to tactical goal.

Pickleball
DAILY COMPANION

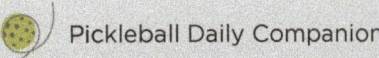

SEPTEMBER 24

When your partner hits a sharp cross-court shot that pulls opponents wide, position yourself outside the court to intercept their return. This surprise attack, called an "Erne," often wins points immediately but requires good timing and communication.

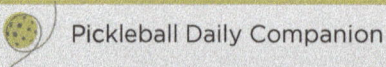

Pickleball Daily Companion

SEPTEMBER 25

When you speed up at the NVZ, prepare for the counter-attack immediately. Position your paddle toward your backhand side and angle it downward. Most speed-ups come back fast and straight. This ready position lets you redirect their return down at their feet instead of getting caught in a flat hitting battle.

SEPTEMBER 26

Level up your game by studying the official pickleball rulebook. Advanced players know clever rules about faults (like when you can step in the kitchen), positioning, and court boundaries that create opportunities many recreational players overlook.

Coach's Tip:

Rule knowledge is your secret weapon.

 Pickleball Daily Companion

SEPTEMBER 27

Use developing skills to create better rallies, not just quick winners. Against newer players, employ techniques that challenge them appropriately while keeping points engaging.

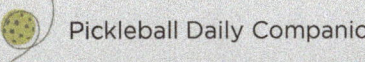

SEPTEMBER 28

Practice new techniques with mindful body awareness. Check in with your energy, balance, and mental focus before attempting complicated shots.

Coach's Tip:

Make every practice a positive experience - joy helps new techniques stick.

 Pickleball Daily Companion

SEPTEMBER 29

Integrate your expanded skills into fluid, natural game flow. The goal is developing sophisticated shots that feel like natural extensions of your game, not forced attempts.

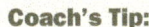

Coach's Tip:

Know the basics first, then add complexity with purpose.

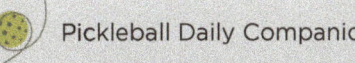

Reflect on how your game has evolved this month. What feels more natural now that used to challenge you? Growth happens gradually - acknowledge progress to build momentum.

Coach's Tip:

The willingness to adapt, learn, and grow through every challenge - that's what turns good players into great ones.

 Pickleball Daily Companion

OCTOBER

Polish your existing abilities to a high shine. Small adjustments in timing, positioning, and technique can create dramatic improvements. This month is about refinement - making your good shots great and your great shots automatic.

OCTOBER 1

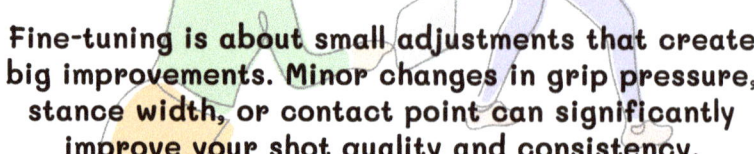

Fine-tuning is about small adjustments that create big improvements. Minor changes in grip pressure, stance width, or contact point can significantly improve your shot quality and consistency.

Coach's Tip:

Make one small technical change at a time and monitor its impact.

 Pickleball Daily Companion

Focus on developing your backhand consistency - it's the key to evening out your game. Players with reliable backhands can't be targeted as easily and have more strategic options available.

 Pickleball Daily Companion

OCTOBER 3

When you're running to reach a ball, stop and split-step before hitting rather than swinging on the run. Players moving at full speed are much more likely to hit balls out or into the net. Take that extra half-second to plant your feet and get balanced.

Pickleball Daily Companion

Pickleball
DAILY COMPANION

OCTOBER 4

Learn to identify player types during matches. The lobber who resets points, the corner-hunter who aims for sharp angles, the cross-court specialist. Recognizing patterns helps you adjust strategy.

Pickleball
DAILY COMPANION

Pickleball Daily Companion

OCTOBER 5

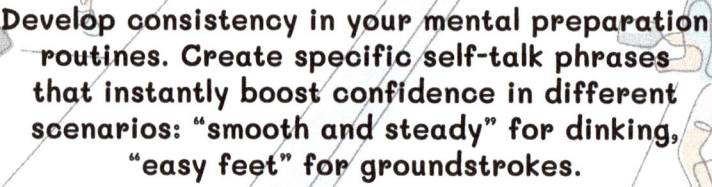

Develop consistency in your mental preparation routines. Create specific self-talk phrases that instantly boost confidence in different scenarios: "smooth and steady" for dinking, "easy feet" for groundstrokes.

OCTOBER 6

Seek out advanced playing partners to observe how they approach the game. Many players have refined something you haven't - their footwork or shot preparation might spark improvements.

 Pickleball Daily Companion

OCTOBER 7

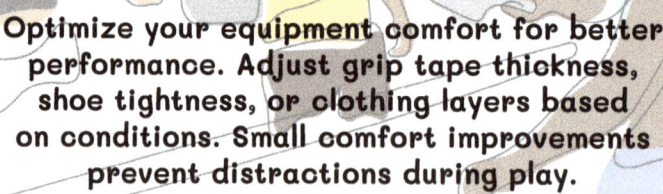

Optimize your equipment comfort for better performance. Adjust grip tape thickness, shoe tightness, or clothing layers based on conditions. Small comfort improvements prevent distractions during play.

OCTOBER 8

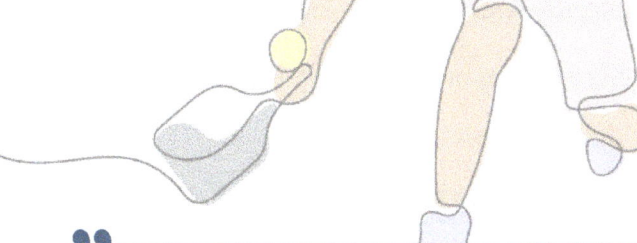

When game pressure increases, notice which shots remain reliable and which break down - this reveals your true strengths.

Coach's Tip:

Develop a quick mental reset routine for pressure moments. Take a breath, focus on one simple cue like 'contact in front,' and commit to that thought.

Pickleball
DAILY COMPANION

Pickleball Daily Companion

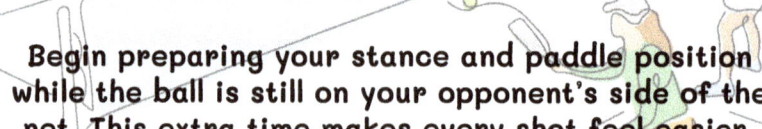

Begin preparing your stance and paddle position while the ball is still on your opponent's side of the net. This extra time makes every shot feel easier.

Pickleball Daily Companion

Pickleball
DAILY COMPANION

OCTOBER 10

Fine-tune your shot selection based on court position. From the kitchen line, prioritize placement over power. From the transition zone, focus on getting to the net safely. From the baseline, aim for depth and consistency.

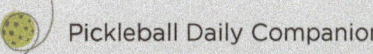

OCTOBER 11

Focus on basic shot sequences. As you become more experienced, you can start to think about your next shot while hitting your current one. Planning one shot ahead helps you position better and make smarter choices.

Pickleball Daily Companion

OCTOBER 12

Build mental flexibility to adapt your game plan during matches. The ability to make strategic adjustments mid-game is a skill that will elevate your play to the next level.

Coach's Tip:
The best game plan is one you can change. Stay committed to winning, yet flexible about how you get there.

Pickleball
DAILY COMPANION

 Pickleball Daily Companion

OCTOBER 13

Suggest games that keep everyone engaged when skill levels vary widely. For instance, a dink-only game with no fast shots until six dinks are hit maintains fun for all levels.

OCTOBER 14

Video yourself playing for five minutes, or have someone capture slow-motion footage of your strokes. Watching later can reveal details you might miss about court positioning, shot patterns, and movement habits.

Pickleball
DAILY COMPANION

Pickleball Daily Companion

OCTOBER 15

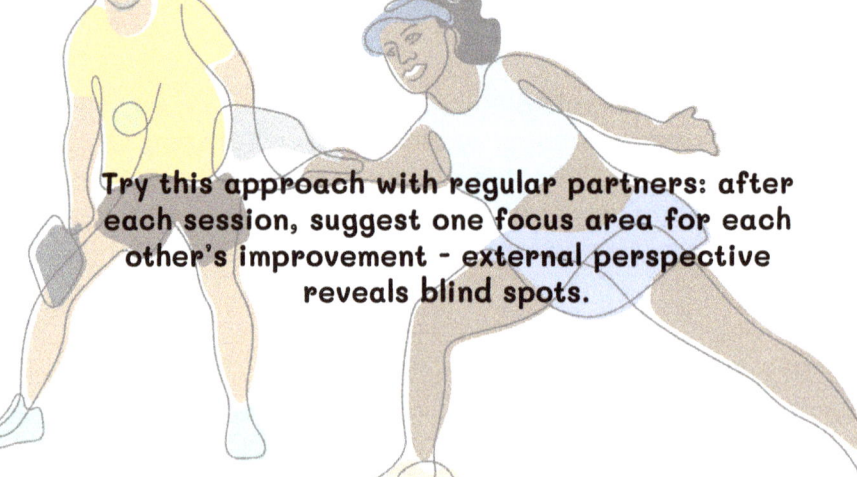

Try this approach with regular partners: after each session, suggest one focus area for each other's improvement - external perspective reveals blind spots.

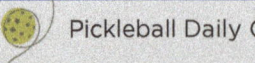
Pickleball Daily Companion

Pickleball
DAILY COMPANION

OCTOBER 16

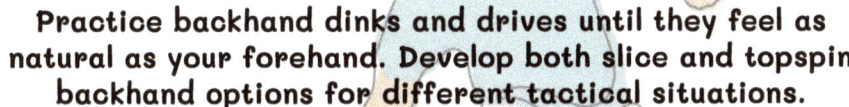

Practice backhand dinks and drives until they feel as natural as your forehand. Develop both slice and topspin backhand options for different tactical situations.

Pickleball
DAILY COMPANION

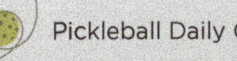
Pickleball Daily Companion

OCTOBER 17

Set tiny, shared goals with partners each session - "let's both call middle balls louder" or "let's move up together after drop shots." Small focuses create rapid improvement.

Coach's Tip:
Some of the best progress comes through micro-improvements. Gracefully refine existing skills before adding completely new ones.

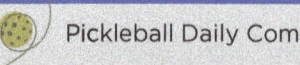

Pickleball Daily Companion

Pickleball
DAILY COMPANION

OCTOBER 18

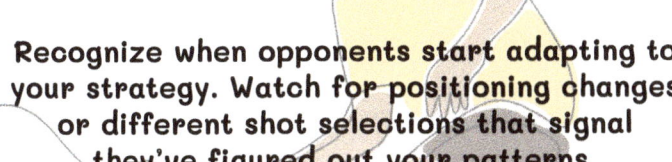

Recognize when opponents start adapting to your strategy. Watch for positioning changes or different shot selections that signal they've figured out your patterns.

Pickleball
DAILY COMPANION

Pickleball Daily Companion

Refine your follow-through direction based on target location. Follow through toward your intended target: cross-court follow-through for cross-court shots, down-the-line follow-through for line shots. Your body knows where you're aiming.

Celebrate pickleball's unique ability to bring generations together. Seek out players from different age groups as partners. Each brings unique skills and perspectives to learn from.

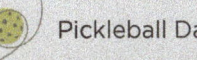

OCTOBER 21

Notice and appreciate small physical improvements - better balance, relaxed shoulders, smoother movement. These wins create mental confidence that accelerates technical growth.

Coach's Tip:

If progress stalls, target flexibility, core stability, and movement efficiency. These small wins fuel confidence and stack up into big breakthroughs.

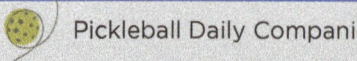
Pickleball Daily Companion

Pickleball
DAILY COMPANION

OCTOBER 22

Notice how your technique changes when you get tired. Maintaining good form when fatigued separates consistent players from streaky ones.

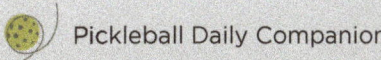

OCTOBER 23

Watch for opponents hitting on the run. Players scrambling at full speed to chase balls frequently send shots long or into the net. Stay patient and let their rushed shots do the work for you.

Coach's Tip:
When you learn to recognize opponent tells like over-aggressive backswings, you can avoid hitting balls that are likely going out.

Pickleball
DAILY COMPANION

OCTOBER 24

Refine your ability to adapt to different partners quickly. Develop communication and positioning concepts that work effectively with any teammate.

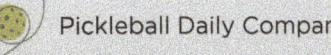

OCTOBER 25

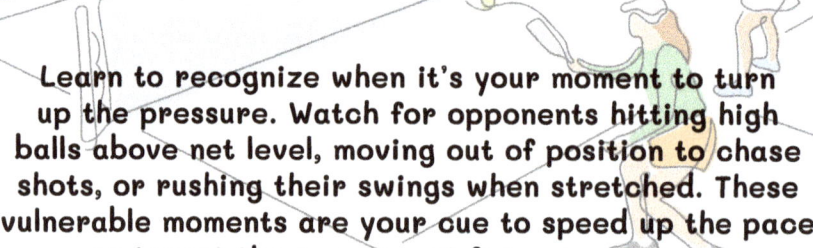

Learn to recognize when it's your moment to turn up the pressure. Watch for opponents hitting high balls above net level, moving out of position to chase shots, or rushing their swings when stretched. These vulnerable moments are your cue to speed up the pace or target the open court for easy winners.

Notice how your improvements affect your partner. Sharper individual play often leads to smoother teamwork and more confident decision-making together.

Pickleball
DAILY COMPANION

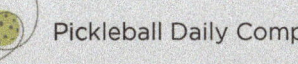

OCTOBER 27

Develop your awareness of how different opponents bring out different aspects of your game. The patient player who makes you focus on placement, the aggressive player who sharpens your defense, the strategic player who challenges your decision-making - each opponent helps refine different skills.

OCTOBER 28

Refine your contact point timing. Hit dinks at the peak of the bounce for control, drives on the rise for pace, and drops slightly after the peak for better arc. Small timing adjustments create big improvements.

Pickleball
DAILY COMPANION

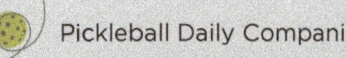

OCTOBER 29

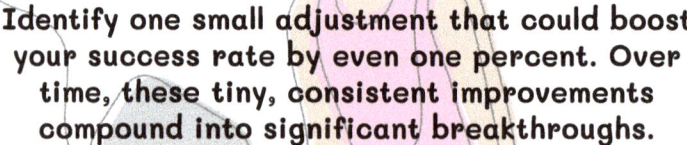

Identify one small adjustment that could boost your success rate by even one percent. Over time, these tiny, consistent improvements compound into significant breakthroughs.

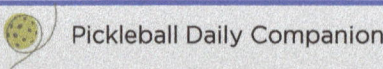

OCTOBER 30

Refine your play with shadow practice - repeating strokes and footwork without a ball, optionally in front of a mirror. This builds mind-body connection, muscle memory, and improves technique before hitting the court.

OCTOBER 31

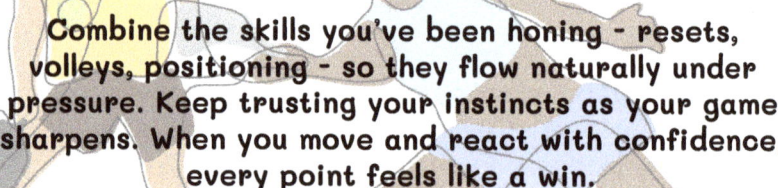

Combine the skills you've been honing - resets, volleys, positioning - so they flow naturally under pressure. Keep trusting your instincts as your game sharpens. When you move and react with confidence, every point feels like a win.

Coach's Tip:
Refinement never ends. It's about continuously finding small ways to make your game more reliable, effective and fun.

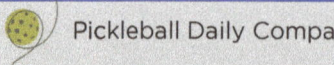
Pickleball Daily Companion

Pickleball
DAILY COMPANION

NOVEMBER

 GRATITUDE & SPORTSMANSHIP

Pickleball gives us so much - friendships that last, laughter that heals, and moments of pure joy. This month, we celebrate the beautiful community we're part of and the grace that makes every game better when we bring our best selves to the court.

NOVEMBER 1

Think about one person pickleball brought into your life this year. Reach out and let them know what their friendship means to you.

Coach's Tip:
Let joy be your compass. Allow your pleasure in playing to guide decisions about frequency, intensity, and types of activities you pursue.

 Pickleball Daily Companion

NOVEMBER 2

Spend a session reinforcing what's already working. Dial in your best shots, build on your strengths, and let confidence carry over to the rest of your game - and your day.

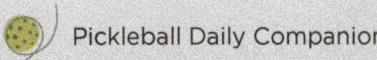

Express genuine appreciation for your partners' contributions. Acknowledge not just their great shots but also their encouragement, patience, and positive attitude.

 Pickleball Daily Companion

NOVEMBER 4

Long rallies create fun for all four players. Quick winners on the serve might feel satisfying, but engaging exchanges are what make pickleball addictive. Patience and smart play let everyone use their skills, make key saves, and enjoy memorable moments. Great rallies bring out everyone's best play.

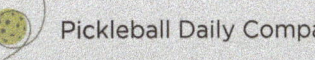

Pickleball Daily Companion

NOVEMBER 5

Focus on the good today. Notice what's working - your footwork, your patience, the rallies you're building. This positive mindset keeps you loose and playing better.

Coach's Tip:
Gratitude is good strategy. When you appreciate the chance to play, pressure turns off and flow turns on.

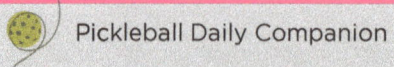
Pickleball Daily Companion

NOVEMBER 6

Appreciate being part of pickleball's uniquely positive culture. Pickleball communities celebrate effort, encourage improvement, and genuinely enjoy each other's success. This supportive environment makes every player better — both on and off the court.

Coach's Tip:
What makes pickleball special? The community where intense rallies and real friendships happen side by side.

Pickleball
DAILY COMPANION

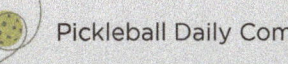

Pickleball Daily Companion

NOVEMBER 7

Cherish your body's ability to play this wonderful sport. When you move without pain, recover quickly, or simply feel strong on court, those are gifts worth celebrating.

NOVEMBER 8

Notice how your positive energy ripples through the court. Your encouragement after great rallies, patience during someone's learning curve, and smiles after tough losses shape positive culture.

Coach's Tip:

Identify players who stay consistently positive. What specific behaviors can you adopt from the most encouraging players you know?

Pickleball
DAILY COMPANION

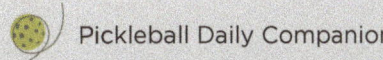

Pickleball Daily Companion

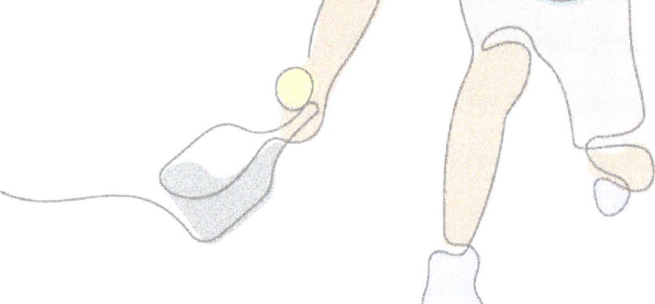

Demonstrate good sportsmanship through your shot selection. Choose shots that challenge appropriately - avoid unnecessary body shots and consider each opponent's mobility when selecting tactics.

NOVEMBER 10

Practice grace during frustrating points, whether they be missed shots, bad bounces, or tough losses. How you handle setbacks sets the tone for everyone around you and often influences future games.

 Pickleball Daily Companion

NOVEMBER 11

Generous line calls create good karma on the court. If one partner thinks it's out, trust that call. Great sportsmanship brings good energy and makes the game better for all.

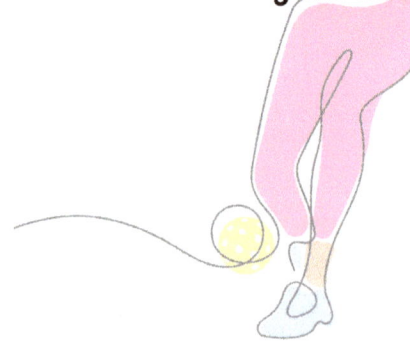

NOVEMBER 12

When facing difficult moments, reconnect with why you love pickleball - this helps you navigate challenges with perspective. Remember the friendships, the movement, the mental stimulation that drew you to the game.

Coach's Tip:

When you're struggling with your game, remember that even challenging days on court offer lessons and connections that enrich your life.

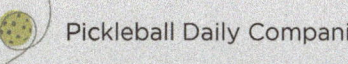
Pickleball Daily Companion

NOVEMBER 13

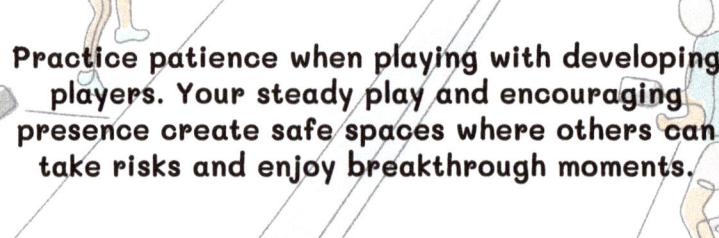

Practice patience when playing with developing players. Your steady play and encouraging presence create safe spaces where others can take risks and enjoy breakthrough moments.

Pickleball
DAILY COMPANION

NOVEMBER 14

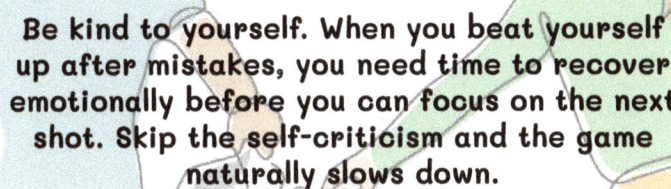

Be kind to yourself. When you beat yourself up after mistakes, you need time to recover emotionally before you can focus on the next shot. Skip the self-criticism and the game naturally slows down.

Coach's Tip:

Don't say to yourself what you wouldn't say to a partner. Avoid thoughts like 'I shouldn't have missed that serve' or 'I can't believe I hit it out again.'

Pickleball
DAILY COMPANION

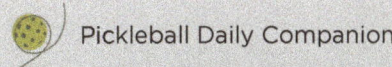
Pickleball Daily Companion

NOVEMBER 15

Reflect on the lessons pickleball has taught you about life. Consider how skills like patience, adaptability, and resilience transfer beyond the court.

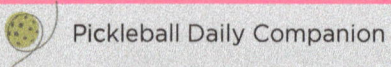

NOVEMBER 16

Try this approach to setbacks: reframe mistakes as "data collection" - necessary development steps rather than failures to avoid.

Pickleball Daily Companion

NOVEMBER 17

Express appreciation for partners who help you improve. Value those who challenge you, encourage you, and create positive learning environments.

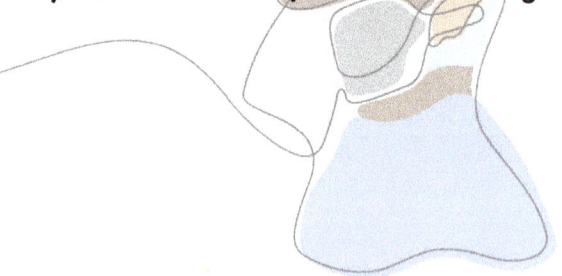

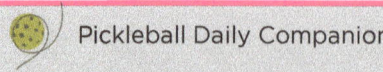

NOVEMBER 18

Practice the same kindness toward yourself that you show your partners. You wouldn't tell a teammate "you're terrible at dinks" after a mistake, so don't say it to yourself either. Gentle self-talk builds confidence and resilience.

 Pickleball Daily Companion

NOVEMBER 19

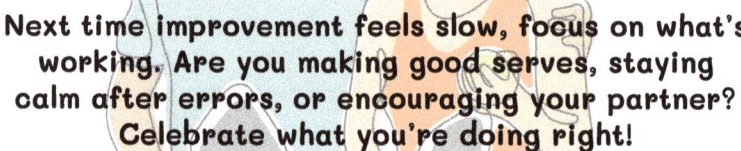

Next time improvement feels slow, focus on what's working. Are you making good serves, staying calm after errors, or encouraging your partner? Celebrate what you're doing right!

NOVEMBER 20

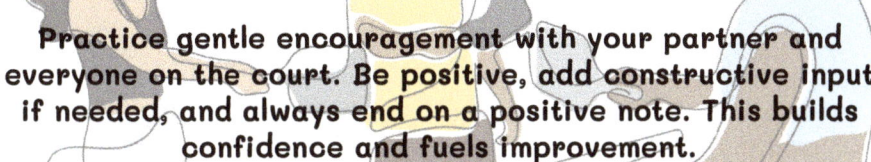

Practice gentle encouragement with your partner and everyone on the court. Be positive, add constructive input if needed, and always end on a positive note. This builds confidence and fuels improvement.

Coach's Tip:
Appreciate difficult moments as much as easy successes.

Pickleball
DAILY COMPANION

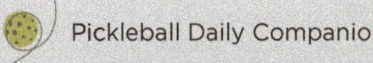

Pickleball Daily Companion

Appreciate how pickleball supports aging gracefully and maintaining vitality. The game provides ongoing physical and mental challenges that support long-term health and community connection.

Appreciate pickleball's joyful simplicity - hitting a little yellow ball with holes back and forth with friends, old and new. Notice the joy in the laughs over missed shots and unexpected winners.

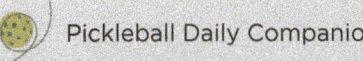

Find satisfaction in your current abilities while working toward future goals. Your serve may not be perfect, but it gets points started. Your dinks may not drop like the pros do', but they create fun rallies.

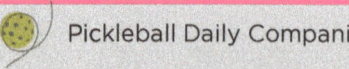

NOVEMBER 24

Thank partners for their patience during your learning process. Pay it forward by offering the same encouragement you received to someone struggling with skills you've developed.

Coach's Tip:

The cycle of support keeps our pickleball community strong. What you give comes back in ways you never expect.

Pickleball
DAILY COMPANION

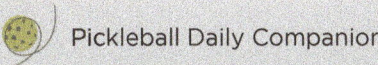

Pickleball Daily Companion

NOVEMBER 25

Practice gratitude for small breakthroughs. When you finally nail that drop shot or stay calm under pressure, pause to appreciate the moment. These mini-victories fuel long-term growth and joy.

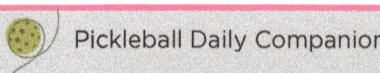

NOVEMBER 26

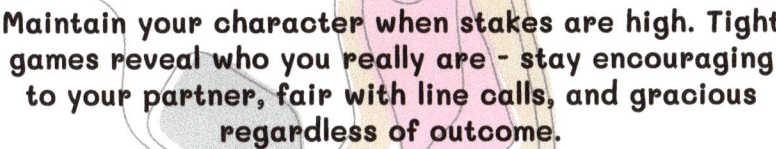

Maintain your character when stakes are high. Tight games reveal who you really are - stay encouraging to your partner, fair with line calls, and gracious regardless of outcome.

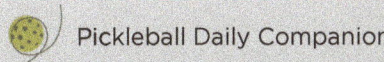

NOVEMBER 27

Take a moment to thank the volunteers and organizers who make pickleball happen in your community. Their hard work setting up courts and running events keeps the game alive and fun for everyone.

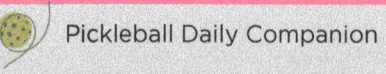
Pickleball Daily Companion

NOVEMBER 28

Remember that your opponents want good competition too. A close, hard-fought match is a gift you give each other - win or lose, everyone gets to play their best.

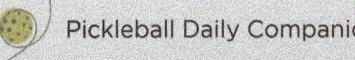

NOVEMBER 29

Reflect on how gratitude has transformed your pickleball experience. When appreciation becomes your default response to challenges and victories, the game becomes less about winning and more about growing.

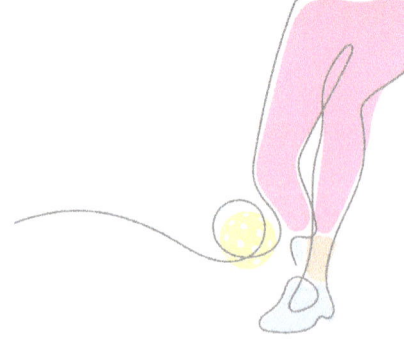

NOVEMBER 30

End November by celebrating the complete pickleball experience. The friendships, laughs, fitness, mental challenges, community connections, and pure joy of great rallies. This sport offers gifts beyond any score.

Coach's Tip:

Gratitude is the foundation of true sportsmanship. When you appreciate the game, opponents, and opportunities, you become the player everyone wants around

 Pickleball Daily Companion

DECEMBER

REFLECTION & GOAL SETTING

Look back on your incredible year of growth and plan for even more improvement ahead. Reflect on lessons learned, celebrate progress made, and set intentions that will guide your pickleball journey into the future.

Pickleball
DAILY COMPANION

DECEMBER 1

As the year winds down, savor the moments that mattered most - the laughter, the joy, and the breakthroughs. Maybe it was landing third-shot drops more consistently, adding spin to your serve, or holding your ground at the net. Each milestone shows how far you've come.

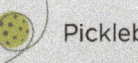

DECEMBER 2

Winter pickleball brings its own magic! If you play on indoor courts, it means softer shots and different rhythms - balls don't bounce as high and move slower than outdoor play. When you can't get to a court, hit against a wall to keep your feel sharp.

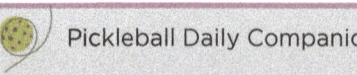

DECEMBER 3

As you plan for next year, consider if your gear still fits your game. Has your paddle weight become too heavy? Do your shoes provide enough lateral support? The right equipment can help you feel stronger, safer, and more at ease on the court.

DECEMBER 4

Continue to build trust through committed reliability. Be the player who shows up mentally and physically. Consistent effort, positive attitude, and dependable play create the foundation for longevity in the sport.

DECEMBER 5

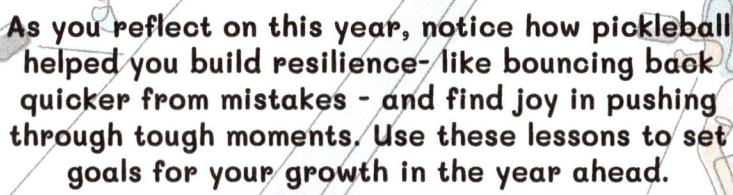

As you reflect on this year, notice how pickleball helped you build resilience- like bouncing back quicker from mistakes - and find joy in pushing through tough moments. Use these lessons to set goals for your growth in the year ahead.

Pickleball
DAILY COMPANION

DECEMBER 6

Honor the friendships and connections pickleball has added to your life this year. From regular partners to tournament teammates to clinic coaches and friends you've trained with, your extended pickleball family has grown in wonderful ways.

 Pickleball Daily Companion

Appreciate how pickleball keeps you moving, laughing, and energized. You're investing in decades of healthy, joyful play by choosing a sport that's both challenging and sustainable.

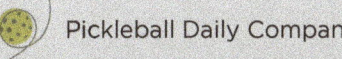

DECEMBER 8

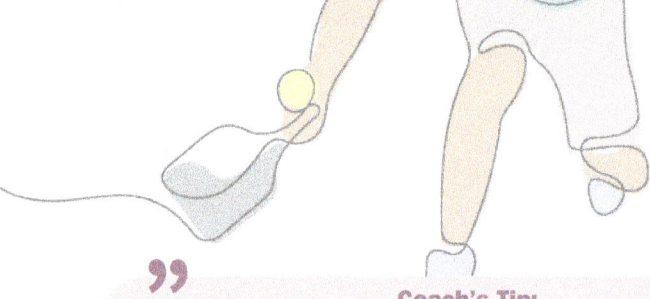

Assess how you've improved with concrete benchmarks. Can you hit seven out of ten serves deep? Land five consecutive dinks in the NVZ? Execute three solid third shot drops? These reveal where to focus practice time.

"

Coach's Tip:

Create monthly skill challenges for next year. "January: improve serve consistency to 8/10." Having measurable goals transforms vague hopes into achievable progress.

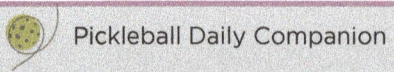

DECEMBER 9

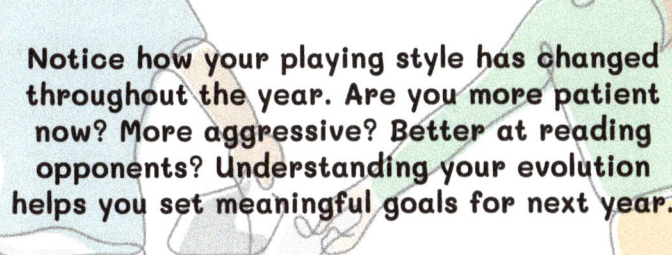

Notice how your playing style has changed throughout the year. Are you more patient now? More aggressive? Better at reading opponents? Understanding your evolution helps you set meaningful goals for next year.

Pickleball
DAILY COMPANION

 Pickleball Daily Companion

DECEMBER 10

As you consider tournament play for next year, remember that etiquette starts with accurate self-assessment. Register for the division that matches your current play, not where you hope to be or where you think you'll easily win.

"

Coach's Tip:

Good sportsmanship means honest skill evaluation - playing up frustrates partners, playing down isn't fair to others.

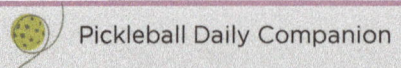

Pickleball Daily Companion

Pickleball
DAILY COMPANION

DECEMBER 11

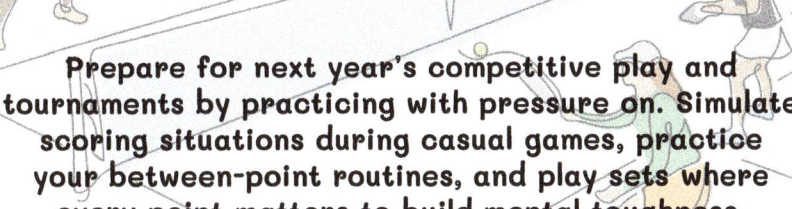

Prepare for next year's competitive play and tournaments by practicing with pressure on. Simulate scoring situations during casual games, practice your between-point routines, and play sets where every point matters to build mental toughness.

DECEMBER 12

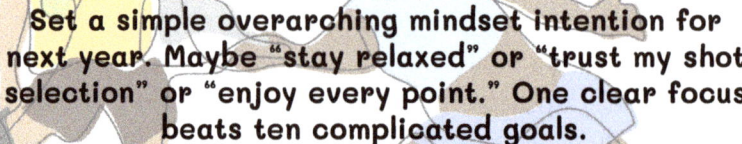

Set a simple overarching mindset intention for next year. Maybe "stay relaxed" or "trust my shot selection" or "enjoy every point." One clear focus beats ten complicated goals.

Coach's Tip:

Your mental game is like a house foundation - everything else depends on its strength, stability, and resilience.

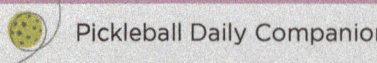
Pickleball Daily Companion

Pickleball
DAILY COMPANION

DECEMBER 13

Learn the art of inclusive leadership on court.
Be welcoming of newcomers with specific
encouragement, organize games that challenge
everyone appropriately, and defuse tension with
humor and perspective.

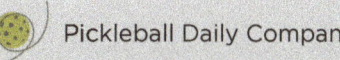

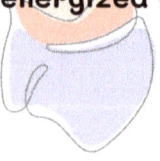

Celebrate how your body has carried you through this amazing year of pickleball! As you plan for next year, think about what makes you feel strongest and most energized on the court.

DECEMBER 15

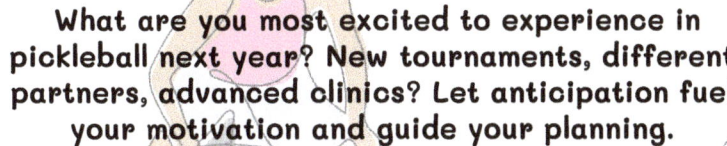

What are you most excited to experience in pickleball next year? New tournaments, different partners, advanced clinics? Let anticipation fuel your motivation and guide your planning.

Pickleball
DAILY COMPANION

Pickleball Daily Companion

DECEMBER 16

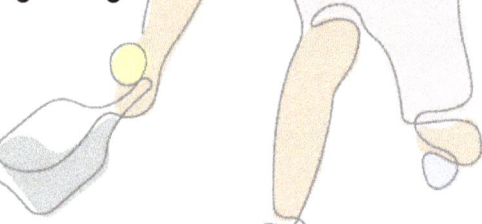

Identify your personal celebration shot - that smooth, confident stroke you can rely on when it matters. Whether it's your cross-court dink or steady serve, having one go-to shot builds confidence.

Coach's Tip:

When you trust one technique completely, it becomes the foundation for taking smart risks elsewhere.

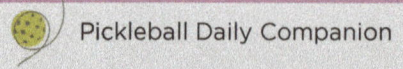
Pickleball Daily Companion

DECEMBER 17

Commit to doing some wall practice next year - even five minutes of dinking against a garage wall builds touch and timing. Solo practice accelerates improvement because you get more repetitions in less time.

Pickleball
DAILY COMPANION

Pickleball Daily Companion

DECEMBER 18

Plan your pickleball bucket list for next year.
What new venues do you want to try? Which
skills excite you most to develop? Having
specific adventures to anticipate keeps
improvement fun and purposeful.

DECEMBER 19

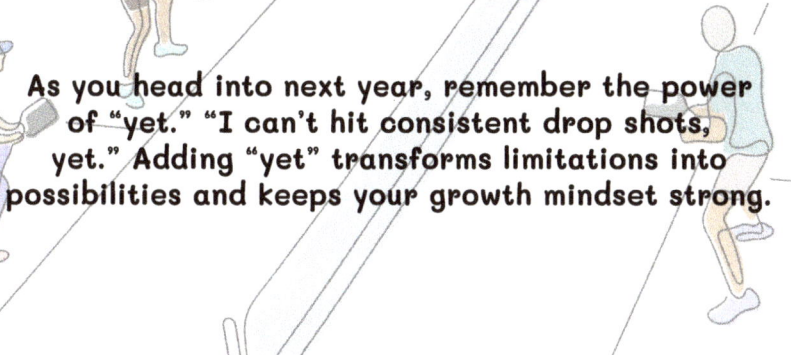

As you head into next year, remember the power of "yet." "I can't hit consistent drop shots, yet." Adding "yet" transforms limitations into possibilities and keeps your growth mindset strong.

Pickleball
DAILY COMPANION

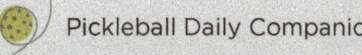

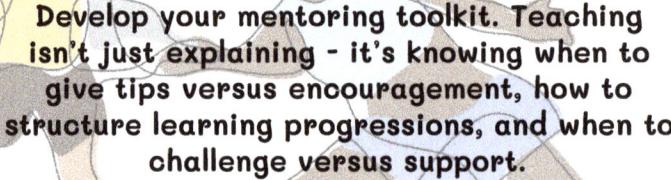

Develop your mentoring toolkit. Teaching isn't just explaining - it's knowing when to give tips versus encouragement, how to structure learning progressions, and when to challenge versus support.

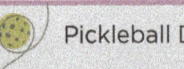
Pickleball Daily Companion

Pickleball
DAILY COMPANION

DECEMBER 21

Commit to playing pickleball for decades, not just months. This long-term view guides smart choices about intensity, recovery, and injury prevention. Sustainable beats spectacular.

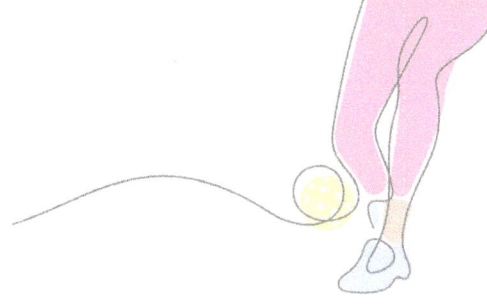

Pickleball
DAILY COMPANION

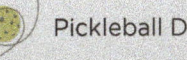

DECEMBER 22

You're not the same player who started this year.
You're more skilled, confident, and connected to the
pickleball community. Set a goal to continue that
growth into next year and beyond.

DECEMBER 23

Create a winter practice routine to maintain your skills. Wall practice for dinks, shadow swings for muscle memory, or balance exercises for footwork. Regular practice sessions, even short ones, maintain muscle memory and keep you game-ready.

Pickleball
DAILY COMPANION

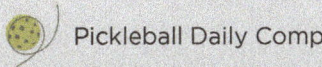

Consider your personal playing philosophy for next year. Are you focused on improvement, social connection, competition, or fitness? Having a clear 'why' guides better decisions about practice, partners, and playing opportunities.

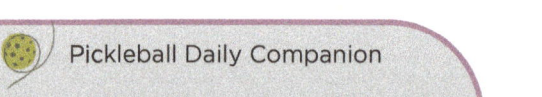

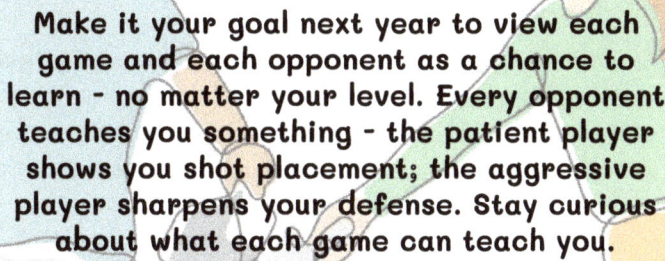

Make it your goal next year to view each game and each opponent as a chance to learn - no matter your level. Every opponent teaches you something - the patient player shows you shot placement; the aggressive player sharpens your defense. Stay curious about what each game can teach you.

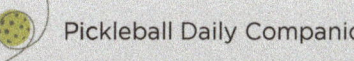

DECEMBER 26

Celebrate pickleball's incredible growth. New courts are appearing everywhere, creating opportunities to discover new venues, make new friends, and maybe even teach some beginner lessons yourself.

 Pickleball Daily Companion

DECEMBER 27

Remember that you're part of something special. The pickleball community provides warmth, encouragement, and shared joy that creates connections enriching your life beyond the court.

Coach's Tip:

Continue contributing to positive culture. Your enthusiasm, kindness, and good sportsmanship help maintain the magic that makes pickleball communities so welcoming.

 Pickleball Daily Companion

DECEMBER 28

Plan to monitor your playing intensity as you view the next year. Adjust your game style if needed - rely more on placement and strategy, less on pure athleticism. Smart adaptation extends playing careers.

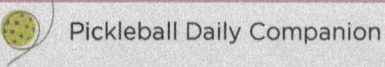

DECEMBER 29

Trust your pickleball instincts going forward. You've developed better judgment about shots, partnerships, and improvement priorities. Your internal compass guides you well.

Pickleball
DAILY COMPANION

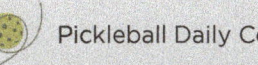

As this year ends, consider how you can give back to the sport that's given you so much. Whether it's welcoming newcomers, organizing games, or sharing what you've learned, your contribution helps grow this amazing community.

Pickleball Daily Companion

Notice how your local court has become more than just a place to play - it's where you've built not just your shots, but your friendships. The connections forged through shared games, encouragement, and laughter create a support system that makes every improvement more meaningful. Pickleball is nothing short of "a once in a century phenomenon." You're part of something truly special.

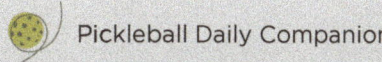

ABOUT THE AUTHOR

Marji Keith is a health coach and passionate pickleball player who's worked on Wall Street, taught windsurfing in the Caribbean, and raised three kids. She believes life's best moments happen when you're moving, learning, and connecting with others - which explains her love for pickleball's perfect blend of strategy, community, and pure fun.

What she loves most about pickleball is that there's always something new to discover - whether it's a technique, strategy, or friendship. That spirit of continuous growth inspired this calendar.

Have thoughts or want to share your own pickleball joy? Reach out at marji@ pickleballdailycompanion.com